coming

together

as readers

SECOND EDITION

DONNA OGLE

coming

together

as readers

BUILDING LITERACY TEAMS

SECOND EDITION

FOREWORD BY
Dorothy Strickland

CORWIN PRESS
A SAGE Publications Company
Thousand Oaks, CA 91320

KH

For information:

Corwin Press
A Sage Publications Company
2455 Teller Road
Thousand Oaks, California 91320
www.corwinpress.com

Sage Publications Ltd.
1 Oliver's Yard
55 City Road
London EC1Y 1SP
United Kingdom

Sage Publications India Pvt. Ltd.
B 1/I 1 Mohan Cooperative
   Industrial Area
Mathura Road, New Delhi 110 044
India

Sage Publications Asia-Pacific Pte. Ltd.
33 Pekin Street #02-01
Far East Square
Singapore 048763

Printed in the United States of America.

Library of Congress Cataloging-in-Publication Data

Ogle, Donna.
Coming together as readers : building literacy teams/Donna Ogle [foreword by Dorothy Strickford]. — 2nd ed.
    p. cm.
Includes bibliographical references and index.
ISBN 978-1-4129-5419-8 (cloth : alk. paper)
ISBN 978-1-4129-5420-4 (pbk. : alk. paper)
   1. Reading—United States. 2. Reading promotion—United States. 3. Community and school—United States. I. Title.

LB1050.O27 2007
372.4—dc22   2006102785

This book is printed on acid-free paper.

07 08 09 10 11 10 9 8 7 6 5 4 3 2 1

Acquisitions Editor:	Hudson Perigo
Editorial Assistant:	Cassandra Harris
Production Editor:	Veronica Stapleton
Copy Editor:	Renee Willers
Typesetter:	C&M Digitals (P) Ltd.
Proofreader:	Joyce Li
Indexer:	Michael Ferreira
Cover Designer:	Monique Hahn

9/3/09

Contents

Foreword

Improving our schools is a top priority at the local, state, and national levels. It is a rare week in which education reform is not featured in our nation's headlines. Educational progress is a topic that engenders opinions from virtually everyone. It is a hot topic of discussion at the political table and at the dinner table. Much of that discussion centers on the most fundamental of all areas of the curriculum—reading education. The focus on reading speaks to the recognition that success in learning to read is essential to achievement in all other areas of the school curriculum. It is also the basis for success in the workplace and key to acquiring personal goals and aspirations. The tension and concern about reading education stems from the fact that many of our school-age students are not succeeding as well as expected. Parents and the public in general want to know why and what can be done about it. Donna Ogle has written an outstanding response to those questions. In *Coming Together as Readers*, Ogle has managed to unpack a complex and multifaceted topic in a way that is immensely straightforward and understandable.

Ogle is highly conversant with the research on best practices in the teaching of reading. Throughout this book, there is evidence of a strong knowledge base that is grounded in the best thinking and scientific inquiry available today. Nevertheless, Ogle gently reminds us that the science of teaching works hand in hand with the art of teaching. Teachers, administrators, and parents should be knowledgeable about their roles in fostering the skills and strategies that support children's learning. Yet, it is the artful application of that knowledge that is required to make learning take hold. We are reminded that teachers and learners are members of several learning communities. The interconnectedness of home, school, and community is an ever-present theme.

An experienced leader and contributor to the field of reading, Ogle brings her ideas to us in a way that speaks directly to teaching and learning. This book is filled with concrete suggestions for improving instruction. But, to her credit, it is her attention to the human quality of the learning equation that stands out and sets this book apart from other books about reading. Ogle goes beyond skills, strategies, and testing to bring the human element back into the topic of learning to read. She helps us see the links and connections among the providers of instruction and what is provided.

Both aspiring and experienced educators will find *Coming Together as Readers* to be immensely helpful as they seek to support the development of readers and writers. As someone who has been a teacher educator in the field of reading for a very long time, this book has helped me to bring the many disparate and sometimes conflicting aspects of the field together with a greater sense of unity and clarity.

Dorothy S. Strickland, PhD
Samuel DeWitt Proctor Professor of Education
The State University of New Jersey

Author's Foreword

I finished the first edition of this book on an October afternoon from my parents' room in a nursing home. As I looked out the window on a bucolic autumn scene, I watched fourth graders led by their teacher troop down the hill to the Care Center. They each had selected favorite books to share with their adopted "grandparents" on their bimonthly visit. Knowing that Brian would soon be at my parents' door, I left so they could share their time together. I love the symbolism of this intergenerational literacy—just what all children and seniors deserve. It seems so natural in a rural community, and then I am reminded of just how much shared literacy occurs in our urban neighborhood in Chicago in the community development project that my husband directs.

Hundreds of volunteers come into our neighborhood every week. Many are university students coming as tutors and Big Brothers and Big Sisters. Others are church people who adopt families, serve in the soup kitchen, or work in the tutoring and afterschool programs. The volunteers who come into the neighborhood are so identified with literacy that when one new church volunteer came into the single-room occupancy hotel for the first time, feeling very uneasy and out of place, he was met with a four-year-old who sidled up to him immediately and asked, "Will you read with me?" The suburban volunteer told others, "I just melted at that request and lost my fear! Of course I could read with her."

One of our former faculty members, Darrell Morris, started a tutoring project for low-achieving primary students from the local school. That Howard Area Tutoring Project is still thriving with the leadership of some outstanding reading specialists and the support of volunteer tutors from the Chicago area. Each year the students in the second grade are tested and the lowest receive one-to-one tutoring twice a week. The coordinated effort of the Howard Area Tutoring Project working with schoolteachers produces much support for the children who have the greatest needs. Just having someone who cares about them and who will sit down and read with them is valuable since most of these children come from single-parent homes where the mothers are overwhelmed with life.

Both in rural mid-America and in more urban environments, literacy can bring people together and extend our shared cultural life. This book is my effort to challenge all of us to think about how we as teachers and educators help stimulate shared literacy. I think it is more important now than ever that we think strategically about how we can make our value of literacy very clear to young people. Reading seems to be competing with more mass media-promoted activities and with computer games for children's leisure time. Since reading is a more individual and internal activity, we have to be self-conscious about how to make it more visible to children in our highly media-dominated environment. We adults may value literacy, but we need to consciously let children see us valuing literacy in our lives for many of them to internalize the value themselves.

Donna Ogle
Chicago

Preface

"To realize the potential of school reform, teachers must not only correlate the multiple dimensions of materials, pedagogy, curriculum, and their beliefs about teaching and learning, but they must also attend to the emotional needs of their students. . . . School reform policy not only should aim to raise test scores, but also should encourage a change of heart about what it means to educate—to help students reach their potential" (Simone, 2001, p. 69).

Coming Together as Readers, second edition, is devoted to the proposition that reading together as colleagues, as families, as members of classroom communities, and as part of our lives as citizens in particular locales is vital to our well-being. By sharing what we learn from our own reading and study as teachers, we build the foundations of our professional and personal growth as educators. When we also create a reading culture within our classrooms, we attend to the emotional and academic needs of our students and create compelling reasons for them to become active, lifelong readers. By providing a variety of ways that students can also share their reading engagements and experiences, we create classrooms and schools identified as reading communities. Attending to both what we teach and how we nurture the joy and value of reading gives us the power to help each child reach his or her potential and meet or exceed set standards. Both are essential parts of our role as teachers and educators.

Chapter 1: "Beginning to Share Literacy" illuminates ways that teachers can make a difference in the reading life of their students and by so doing make a positive impact on their professional growth. Central to the discussion in Chapter 1 is the importance of the social nature of literacy. If we want students to become readers for life, we can help start them on that road by sharing our own engagement as members of reading groups. As teachers, we are powerful role models for the students we teach. We begin the book by providing some mirrors to our own influence on our students by the indirect ways we do or do not model the value of reading in our lives as adults, individually and corporately. It is like the old adage, what we do speaks so loudly our students can't hear what we say. This chapter offers some guides for thinking about those subtle messages we communicate about reading and about the potential for enhancing the shared nature of literate communities. We make a difference in the literacy of our students in many ways. The reading audit provided at the end of the chapter is a powerful tool to use to make the self-reflection a community activity. It includes the range of ways we need to think together and create an optimal commitment to the importance of reading for all students.

Chapter 2: "Teachers Working Together" presents some examples and hopefully will stimulate some new visioning of possibilities for teams of teachers to come together to deepen a shared understanding and develop more forceful programs of reading instruction for students. Many exciting changes are taking place in schools as the power of learning communities is verified in both teacher reflections and empirical studies of schools where students have been able to achieve well beyond similar students in other comparable schools. By the single factor of being in a school committed to teachers as learners, we are more likely to become effective teachers. This is powerful! Examples in the chapter explore ways schools are creating teams of teachers who share literacy together, both for personal enjoyment and to improve instruction. Teachers who are active and engaged as readers and learners have a positive impact on their students. Many suggestions are included for ways to create professional communities both within and beyond school boundaries; the message is that we can all take steps in this direction and that many resources are available to help in reaching the goal.

Chapter 3: "Building a Literacy Community in the Classroom" focuses on the central community in most teachers' lives—their classroom. Hopefully, readers will think about the tangible ways they have already nurtured reading communities and use this chapter to explore the several different dimensions that are possible in classrooms that invite literacy. Perhaps some new approach or added visible incentive will make it possible to reach even more children! This chapter begins by exploring the first thing students see as they enter their classroom—the physical environment. Does it look like a place for reading? Then attention shifts to the students. What is special about each of them, and what is likely to motivate them to read? The issue of motivation is important, and a section focuses on adolescents since nurturing them to develop as readers is more challenging than starting primary children on the path of reading. The importance of the range of literacy materials and activities is then explored. Teachers connect students with literacy by including a wide variety of materials in the classroom and by giving student writing and responses to literacy a dominant place in the room. The important role teachers play as models of literacy, as we share our literacy and also read to students, is not overlooked. It is also important to think of what we can do to encourage students to develop the habit of sharing their own responses to reading with classmates. Finally, ideas are provided for maximizing the impact of other adults in the room and sponsoring special events for the whole class.

Chapter 4: "Working Together With Students' Families" focuses on ways to build good partnerships with our students' families. Think about what schools are doing to make families feel welcome and involved. There may be many initiatives under way. There may be exciting things going on that we all can learn from. The chapter begins by first suggesting we give some attention to the communities represented so we do not proceed as if all families share our values and cultural assumptions. Central to reaching the communities and families of students is sending clear messages that families are important and are welcomed as part of the school. Creating an inviting school where families feel comfortable participating deserves some special attention, so the chapter outlines some specific roles volunteers can play and ways they can be part of the school and classroom life. Then we look more specifically at ways families can become part of the academic life of the classroom and be involved in monitoring student work and evaluations, especially during conferences. With the increasing mobility of families within the United States and around the world, we have highlighted some special programs that schools have developed that respond to those particular needs.

Chapter 5: "Working Together at the School Level" draws our attention to the powerful resources students are for one another and the importance of seeing literacy as something that identifies the whole school and is tangibly shared, celebrated, and visible to all. The pressure for testing and discrete content outcomes must not overwhelm our goal of empowering students to be in charge of their own learning and to become more self-confident as a result of their school experiences. It is also important that students see books and literacy as part of our celebrations, as something to share with others, and that over the years they develop their capacity to contribute positively to a literate world. Several enjoyable suggestions for how schools are doing this are included. In addition, the chapter explores ways students can be important resources for one another through cross-age tutoring and all-school literacy events. Perhaps they will stimulate all of us to recall something we did in the past or some ideas that other schools have tried. We cannot do everything at once, but often some reenergized attention to reading together can be special. In addition, this chapter highlights some ways school professional teams can create an all-school commitment to making literacy enjoyable, a part of the school community, and visible for all those associated with the school.

Chapter 6: "Collaborating With State Departments of Education" was contributed by Eunice Ann Greer, PhD, formerly with the Illinois State Board of Education. She details how state departments of education shape, inform, and support reading improvement. Dr. Greer gives specific ways individual teachers can have an impact on their teaching through involvement with state agencies. Often teachers and administrators have overlooked or felt distant from the state resources. With the increased attention to reading in our society, the role of the state agencies in providing direction and support for school reading programs becomes even more important. The financial resources that are available through Reading First (No Child Left Behind) for state departments of education to coordinate and distribute to local districts requires a partnership among these levels. State standards, required annual assessments in reading, and higher expectations that all students become readers are added incentives for collaboration. Knowledge of the roles and functions of the state educational agencies is important for teachers, and this chapter provides information not readily available elsewhere. In this chapter, we have listed many resources that are available, including Web sites for federal government, state agencies, and professional organizations.

Chapter 7: "Working Together With Communities, Cultures, and the World" begins by exploring ways we can make community literacy more evident and real to students. Literacy takes place beyond the school walls as well as within them. Readers are not only students but also members of the community. Making this reality clear to children is an important part of our task given the rushed lives we all live now. Children need to understand and value literacy as part and parcel of life itself. By bringing the community into the school and by connecting students to reading programs beyond the school, we can help deepen that value in a natural and enjoyable way. Literacy is part of the fabric of our shared lives together. Examples of how to maximize the wealth of resources that are available to us are provided. In the next section, ways community members and organizations provide resources for literacy development are explored. Finally, suggestions for how to connect with business and professional community efforts to support literacy and contacts for several organizations are offered. A wealth of support is available to us beyond our schools.

COMING TOGETHER

Because the focus of this book is on helping teachers make a difference in the literacy lives of their students and communities, real case studies are offered as Coming Together features in each chapter. The practical, proven ways that teachers have come together as readers to make a difference, both personally and professionally, are impressive. These examples from teachers can stimulate thinking, provide practical classroom practice ideas, and help develop an even greater vision of what can be. As readers, we can use this opportunity to reflect on the chapter and put it into the context of our own practice and experience. We might even employ the think/pair/share technique, formulating answers to the open-ended questions and sharing our ideas with colleagues or study groups.

ACKNOWLEDGMENTS

This book is truly a team effort. When Jean Ward asked me to write it, I wasn't sure I could find the space in my busy schedule as an International Reading Association (IRA) officer. However, the more we talked the more she stimulated my interest in sharing what I have been learning as I work with the reading community in Illinois where I live and with the larger worldwide community of educators I have met during my travels and consulting work over the past several years. When we came up with the idea of including the actual voices of some of those outstanding leaders and describing their work, I decided to go ahead. Much of the writing was done at a very stressful point in my life. It was the special cross-generational community created by Karen Mead, fourth grade teacher in Stanton, Iowa, and Bonnie Newton, activities director at the Stanton Care Center, whose inspiration during the hard days I spent with my father in his final year of life sustained me in a special way. I still could not have completed the project without an incredibly helpful and supportive group of colleagues and friends who helped collect information, draft sections, and provide critical feedback.

My first thanks go to my professional colleagues who are engaged daily in creating communities of readers in creative and thoughtful ways. I hope all who gain from this book will appreciate the years of dedication represented in the examples they have shared from their work. Those who contributed the pieces for the Coming Together features that are interspersed throughout the chapters are Karl Androes of the Whirlwind Partnership; Debbie Brown, Mike Dunn, Debbie Gurvitz, and Pat McCarthy (all teachers and members of the Reading Leadership Institute); Karen Mead, Nancy Merel, Roger Passman, Debbie Sheffrin, Janet Steiner O'Malley, Joanne Radliff, Scott Waller, and Suzanne Zweig,

Special thanks to Eunice Greer and her daughter Megan, who were willing to find time in their busy lives for Eunice to write Chapter 6 on the importance of our state departments of education as part of our literacy efforts. I love the continuing stream of fresh ideas and possibilities Eunice thinks of—for the next edition of this book.

Susan Jones was invaluable in helping me find the materials I needed for the book and for writing descriptions of some of the special projects. As part of the Everybody Reads Fluency Project Team and a parent with great insight into adolescent students' motivation her contributions are significant.

A voice I heard throughout the writing of this book and examples of whose work I share is that of John Logan, District 27, Northbrook, Illinois, former assistant superintendent, a great friend, and IRA board member. If he were still with us, he would have been an even greater contributor.

Finally, many thanks to Peggy Kulling, who edited the first edition, and Renee Willers, the guiding editor of this second edition. Their insights and contributions have made this a clearer and stronger book.

Corwin Press would like to thank the following peer reviewers for their editorial insight and guidance:

Lyndon Oswald
Principal
Sandcreek Middle School
Idaho Falls, Idaho

Paulette Moses
5th Grade Teacher, NBCT
Educator
Irmo, SC

Kandace Klenz
Teacher
Peninsula Elementary
Moses Lake, Washington

Ken Schofield
Principal
Chaparral Elementary School
Phoenix, AZ

Jill Denson
Elementary Ed. 1st grade
Millard Public Schools
Omaha, Nebraska

Sharon Neff

About the Author

 Donna Ogle is a professor of reading and language at National-Louis University in Chicago, Illinois. She served as president of the International Reading Association 2001–2002, and as executive officer from 1999–2001. Donna teaches graduate courses in literacy, and engages in research and staff development projects in the United States and internationally. She served as a project coordinator and staff developer in Russia and other eastern European countries as part of the Reading and Writing for Critical Thinking Project (RWCT) from 1999–2003. She also served as a consultant to the U.S. Agency for International Development Centers for Excellence in Teacher Training in Central America and the Andean region She also consulted in the Dominical Republic with RWCT.

Donna's primary areas of work are reading and learning strategies and the process of instructional change in schools, especially those in urban areas. She is currently directing a middle school literacy project (Project ALL—Advancing Literacy for Learning) in the Chicago Public Schools (Chicago Community Trust funding) and is a director of the Transitional Literacy Project funded by the McDougal Family Foundation. As part of the U.S. government Adventures of the American Mind Project for university faculty development, she is collaborating on ways to use the American Memory resources of the Library of Congress in teacher education. Donna has also coordinated the development of an Administrators' Academy for Literacy 4–8 through a grant from the Illinois State Board of Education.

Donna has written widely and is also featured on many videotape programs (ASCD & IRI Skylight), Her latest books are *All Children Read*, Second Edition, coauthored with Charles Temple, P. A. Crawford, and P. Freppon (2008; published by Allyn & Bacon); *Coming Together as Readers*, 1st ed. (2002; published by Skylight Professional Books); and *Reading Comprehension: Strategies for Independent Learners*, coauthored with Camille Blachowicz (2001; published by Guilford).

She and Camille Blachowicz are coeditors of a series of books for teachers, *Tools for Teaching Literacy*, being published by Guilford Press. In that series she coauthors a book *Tools for Integrating Instruction: Literacy and Science* with Judy McKee. She is also an author of the *Reading Toolkit for Social Studies* (2004) with Bill McBride, senior consultant for McDougal-Littell's history text, *Creating America* (2000; published by McDougal-Littell), and a senior consultant for their forthcoming secondary literature series.

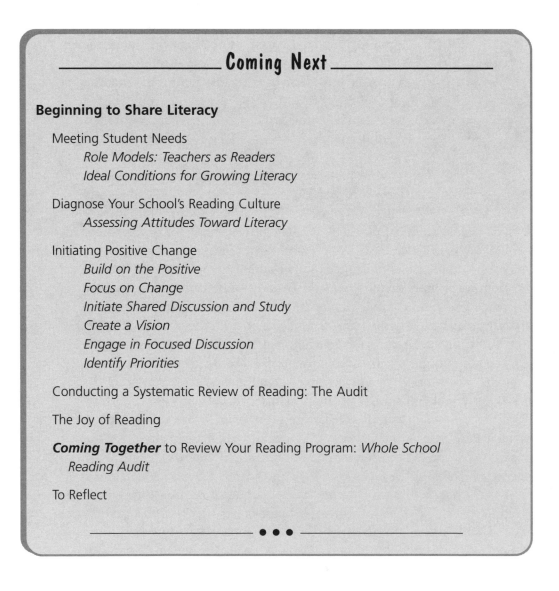

Coming Next

Beginning to Share Literacy

Meeting Student Needs
    Role Models: Teachers as Readers
    Ideal Conditions for Growing Literacy

Diagnose Your School's Reading Culture
    Assessing Attitudes Toward Literacy

Initiating Positive Change
    Build on the Positive
    Focus on Change
    Initiate Shared Discussion and Study
    Create a Vision
    Engage in Focused Discussion
    Identify Priorities

Conducting a Systematic Review of Reading: The Audit

The Joy of Reading

Coming Together to Review Your Reading Program: *Whole School Reading Audit*

To Reflect

Beginning to Share Literacy

MEETING STUDENT NEEDS

Learning to read is a lifetime journey. Right from the start, we need a great deal of nurturing and support to enjoy the challenge and find successes along the way. Our families are our first literacy teachers. It is often from those warm memories of being read to while in a parent's lap that children make a personal connection to reading. Research has shown how important the first few years of life are in establishing the language and cognitive foundations for later learning. It is also true that the experiences children have in early elementary grades are crucial in developing the skills and strategies as well as the successes that help them become confident readers. This is just the beginning. Young readers need to continue to develop and expand their reading strategies for the wide range of reading tasks and contexts they will experience in life. The more teachers work together and link literacy beyond the school, the more likely all students will continue to see the importance of reading in life and to stay motivated lifelong readers.

Reading, a seemingly private activity, is actually a social experience. The time spent engaged with a text is individual, but the purposes and motivations that bring readers and texts together are deeply rooted in social and contextual experiences. Children who come from communities where families value reading and nurture them from infancy into a reading culture generally become able readers (National Assessment of Educational Progress [NAEP], 2004). Children not so fortunate, who live in homes with poorly educated parents, surrounded by a culture devoid of books and print, are at risk for school failure (Neuman, Celano, Greco, & Shue, 2001).

Schools also create environments that have both positive and negative effects on students' literacy development. The impact of schools is substantial. In fact, the 2001 Program for International Student Assessment (PISA) study (Organisation for Economic Co-operation and Development) comparing literacy levels of 15-year-olds in 34 countries concluded that school efficacy can override low socioeconomic conditions in the development of reading ability (Organisation for Economic Co-operation and Development [OECD], 2001). Other studies done within the United States confirm these findings.

We as educators enhance our effectiveness in helping students develop as readers when we attend both to the social contexts we create in the school and to the instruction we provide (Guthrie, 2000; Oldfather, 1995). Everyone benefits when teachers, administrators, and paraprofessionals come together and create learning communities within the school (Center for Improving Early Reading Achievement [CIERA], 2001; WestEd, 2000). This is a significant finding. Data from these school efficacy studies confirm that teachers who together engage in examining ways to solve instructional problems and adjust their teaching to more effectively meet students' needs are able to help students learn more and become better readers.

Current expansion of the role of literacy teams in schools and the use of literacy coaches reflect the growing awareness of the importance of collaboration and cooperation at the school level. In many schools teachers, library media specialists, English as a Second Language (ESL) and special education teachers are part of this team. The Regular Education Initiative has created an important incentive for special education teachers to collaborate as part of the regular instructional team efforts. No longer can teachers work alone in creating rich reading experiences for all their students; cooperative efforts are critical. School teams meet regularly, develop shared goals and procedures, monitor student achievement, and problem-solve issues related to providing the instructional experiences students need. Support professionals are in the classroom working alongside the classroom teacher attending to students' learning and social needs. This new shared instruction creates incentives for teachers to develop shared expertise. Professional development is ongoing as teams study together and continue to refine instructional practice to provide the differentiated programs demanded by students' needs.

There is a lot expected of schools today. Many faculties continue to evolve as learning communities. No two settings are exactly alike in how they create their own blueprints for effectiveness. School cultures are palpable and powerful. A lively, literate culture is easy to identify. Books, magazines, and student-constructed messages are everywhere. Teachers share what they read both personally and professionally. Students enjoy reading a wide range of materials and have their own favorites. Supports are in place for those needing additional instruction and adapted assignments. The schools take advantage of all resource personnel available—professional and volunteer. Parents and the community are part of the support for and celebration of reading.

Role Models: Teachers as Readers

An important foundation for developing a literate culture in a school is taking seriously the power of adults as role models of readers and inquiring learners. Students are much more likely to take literacy seriously and make it a central part of their lives if they see their teachers enjoying and reaping the benefits of shared literacy. In addition, when teachers study together and engage in school-based professional development, students learn more of the lifelong value of reading as a way to learn and grow. And the impact on student achievement is also positive when teachers learn together, both by providing real role models of active learners and through the fruits of such study in the higher-quality literacy instruction teachers then provide.

With the rush of contemporary life, with many adults spending little time relaxing at home, children have few opportunities to see adults reading and enjoying it. Teachers can play an important role by consciously modeling what it means to be a reader. One of the easiest and best ways teachers have of sharing their interest in literacy is to read aloud to students. As Jim Trelease (2001) explained, "Every time we read aloud to a child or class, we're giving a commercial for the pleasures of reading" (p. 36). Teachers read from their own personal favorites, from student texts, and from materials that are just above the students' own comfort level.

Teachers serve as models of good readers for students by sharing experiences that come from professional study. Because adult reading is generally so invisible, we need to make special efforts to tell students about how we use reading to become better teachers. When taking graduate courses, some teachers bring their textbooks and professional magazines to their classrooms and tell students about what they are reading and show the course materials. Some ask students for their input on ideas they are learning, and some students serve as sounding boards for the new ideas. For example, one teacher shared the following with her class: "I have just read about having students do partner reading instead of oral whole class reading of the text. The authors of the article say it can give students a chance to read more and that they like it better. What do you think? Should we try it?" The response was great; the class conducted its own research and decided that they wanted to add partner reading to their routine.

Being aware of and sharing more about our own reading, our participation in adult shared reading activities, our frustrations when we can't find time to read, and our delight at finding interesting tidbits we have learned from reading can all help our students see the role reading plays in the lives of adults. Most adults read regularly (Smith, 2000)—on the job, for personal learning, for keeping up with current events, and for spiritual support. However, many adults admit to finding little time for personal reading (Scholastic, 2006). Helping students know about the benefits of being a good reader is one of our responsibilities. With the competing demands for children's time, it is important that reading as a personal choice be supported strategically. We can do this in a variety of ways, many more of which will be discussed in following chapters.

Ideal Conditions for Growing Literacy

The International Reading Association's (IRA) "Making a Difference Means Making It Different" (2000) provides a research-based summary of what we know about good instruction and climate in schools that promote literacy. It is intended as a guide for formulating educational policy and improving practice. When teachers and administrators meet together and discuss how well the conditions included in the 10 IRA Reading Rights (see Figure 1.1) reflect the local characteristics and, which are not representative, topics for further inquiry can easily be determined.

DIAGNOSE YOUR SCHOOL'S READING CULTURE

Teachers often wonder about the degree to which their schools have created a culture that encourages students to become readers. If you want to check to see if there are some additional ways you might strengthen support for reading in your school, you may want to use some of the tools that follow, including conducting a staff survey of the literacy climate in your building. You might want to try the simple, easy-to-administer survey (see Figure 1.2) as a way to begin a conversation among the staff.

Assessing Attitudes Toward Shared Literacy

Take stock of your school and think about where there is shared literacy among the adults by answering the following questions:

(continued on page 7)

International Reading
Association (IRA) Reading Rights

Children have a right to

- early reading instruction based on individual needs
- reading instruction that builds the skill and desire to read increasingly complex materials
- well-prepared teachers who keep their skills current through professional development
- access to a wide variety of books and other reading material in classroom, school, and community libraries
- reading assessment that identifies their strengths as well as their needs and involves them in making decisions about their own learning
- receive intensive instruction from professionals specifically prepared to teach reading
- reading instruction that involves parents and communities in their academic lives
- reading instruction that makes meaningful use of their first language skills
- equal access to the technology used for the improvement of reading instruction

SOURCE: From Making a Difference Means Making It Different, Honoring Children's Rights to Excellent Reading Instruction: A Position Statement of the International Reading Association (2002). Reprinted with permission of the International Reading Association. Retrieved February 15, 2007, from http://www.reading.org/resources/issues/positions_rights.html

All students have a right to

- instruction that builds the skill and desire to read increasingly complex materials
- access to a wide variety of reading materials that appeal to their interests
- assessment that shows their strengths as well as their needs

Adolescent learners have a right to

- access a wide variety of reading materials that appeal to their interests
- instruction that builds the skill and desire to read increasingly complex materials
- assessment that shows their strengths as well as their needs
- expert teachers who model and provide explicit instruction across the curriculum
- reading specialists who assist students having difficulty learning how to read
- teachers who understand the complexities of individual adolescent readers
- homes and communities that support the needs of adolescent learners

Figure 1.1 International Reading Association (IRA) Reading Rights

SOURCE: Adapted from "Adolescent Literacy," a position statement for the Association on Adolescent Literacy of the International Reading Association. © 1999 by the International Reading Association.

Shared Literacy Survey

Directions: Read each of the statements and then indicate whether you think it characterizes your school never, sometimes, usually, or always. When you have finished your survey, compare your responses with those of others. Find areas of strength (scores of usually and always) and areas that you might want to identify as potentially useful to develop (never or sometimes).

	Never	Sometimes	Usually	Always
1. Teachers regularly talk with each other about instruction and share what they are reading professionally.				
2. Students see their teachers discussing what they read from newspapers, professional articles, and books.				
3. Teachers, librarians, and other adults read to students in their own and other classes.				
4. Reading specialists, librarians, and other adults participate in discussion of reading.				
5. Students share their own literacy across classrooms and grade levels (readers' theater, favorite authors, results of inquiry projects, etc.).				
6. Students share with each other what they read independently.				
7. Students engage in paired and/or buddy reading.				
8. Students participate in small group literature discussions in and across classes.				
9. The classroom provides options for how students will respond to and share what they read.				
10. Students learn to help others become better readers across grades.				
11. Students donate books and magazines as special gifts.				

Figure 1.2   Shared Literacy Survey

- Is the faculty meeting a time when teachers and administrators talk about professional articles they have recently read?
- Do faculty make copies of good articles and share them with others?
- Are personal favorite books talked about?
- Do teachers meet together either regularly or periodically to talk about adult books or new children's and adolescent books?
- Are there needs you have that are not being met now? Can you articulate these needs and begin to build to a shared desire for a more collegial professional team?
- If your school does not have a culture where teachers share their literacy and work together as professional learners, then you may want to create a vision for a new way of functioning in the future. This should be a shared endeavor, so be sure there is discussion and questioning among either a grade level team or a group of interested teachers. Are there needs that are not being met now? Can you articulate these needs and begin to build a shared desire for a more collegial professional team?

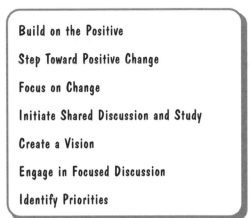

Build on the Positive

Step Toward Positive Change

Focus on Change

Initiate Shared Discussion and Study

Create a Vision

Engage in Focused Discussion

Identify Priorities

INITIATING POSITIVE CHANGE

As you begin to raise awareness of the school culture, make a list of possible ways to initiate new activities. Following are a few possibilities to help you begin.

Build on the Positive

Analyze the faculty and administration and the current situation of the school. Create a chart for your use listing the positive and negative factors that might influence how you could develop a more shared professional culture in the school (see Figure 1.3).

Focus on Change

Think of an area of your reading program that is changing. Where there is a change in the program, the chance to find positive energy to

Force Field Analysis

Factors Working FOR More Professional Engagement Together	Factors Working AGAINST More Professional Engagement Together
1. open atmosphere for ideas	1. full agenda of school activities
2. teachers with interest in learning	2. finding time to meet
3. many new faculty	

Neutral Factors

1. teachers generally satisfied

2. feeling of stability

3. state assessments are okay

Figure 1.3   Force Field Analysis

discuss it together is greater than in other areas. It may be new materials, new assessments, and new attention to integration of curriculum areas. Capture the need of teachers to understand the new area better and suggest some joint meetings.

Initiate Shared Discussion and Study

Is the staff tired of the way staff development days are being used? In many schools there have been too many one-day institutes with outside speakers who never seem to really address the building issues. If this is the case, propose an alternative experiment. Suggest using those days for shared discussion and study. Select a topic that is of high interest in the district, find a few articles that faculty could read, and plan creative use of the time. Or bring a group of teachers together and have each contribute a favorite professional article. Take turns discussing these over several meetings. IRA has provided useful kits for teacher study groups on key topics. These can be previewed by accessing their Web address, www.reading.org.

Create a Vision

An important part of developing a clear shared direction for the school is to create a vision for reading. This can be a part of a literacy team activity or something that emerges from schoolwide professional development and goal setting. An important starting place is identifying the goals and expectations of the adults in the building. Assess the staff and think of the grade-level team or other small group that might share common interests and concerns. Is there some group that might be a pilot for some deeper reflection together? Often it takes a few risk takers to try something new, and then others will follow.

Engage in Focused Discussion

There are good books that lay out the experiences of other schools that have made significant improvements in their literacy. Read one of these together and discuss what teachers think of as most similar to your school and what new approaches and ideas might be worth trying. It can also be useful to take a group of your faculty and administrators to visit another school where teachers engage together as learners. Attend one of their professional development seminars, so your colleagues can see what the possibilities are. Many times people have never seen professionals engaged in academic or literacy-related focused discussion. Create a vision for them.

Identify Priorities

The current attention to assessment provides a clear starting place for discussions of school and grade level commitments to and focus on reading. What has state and local testing indicated about the students' achievement. What areas of literacy need more attention? Which children (grade levels or subgroups) are not keeping up with the general achievement of the school? How engaged are students in reading activities? What does book circulation of school and classroom libraries reveal?

It is also valuable to get an indication of where teachers also are spending their energies Use the survey of belief statements about learning (see Figure 1.4) as a catalyst to get teachers talking about their priorities. In this activity, teachers first identify their top three statements and then come together in groups of three to try to identify shared priorities. From that a whole group discussion can lead to productive clarification of priorities and values in literacy. The list of statements in Figure 1.4 reflects one school where balancing fiction and informational text was important to many.

The Anticipation Guide (Figure 1.5) can be used to stimulate a discussion of shared priorities and commitments to literacy or as a lead-in to a study of reading in your school. The Anticipation Guide can facilitate the sharing of perspectives by the entire faculty. Think about your own situation. You might get discussion going by using the guide provided here or by creating your own set of statements that could lead to a productive exchange among your faculty and administration. By using these tools, students' levels of literacy and teachers' instructional priorities can be compared and new directions jointly determined by school staff.

CONDUCTING A SYSTEMATIC REVIEW OF READING: THE AUDIT

The audit tool of a district or school reading program can start a discussion about the school's reading program and set goals to move forward with new ideas. See Coming Together to Review Your Reading Program at the end of this chapter for a sample audit designed to be used in Illinois schools by their school improvement teams. In this context, audit implies a systematic review of reading. Six sections cover all aspects of the program. Whole school faculty and administrators can use the audit tool to guide a review of the reading program and supportive resources.

THE JOY OF READING

Those of us who love to read and write do so because we belong to communities where literacy is a joy and gives us access to friends, information, support, and stretching. As teachers, we read for our own pleasure and to learn. We know that there is a lot to be gained by connecting with other teachers and educators through their writing. An important part of our literacy is sharing it with others. We read and then talk with our colleagues about the ideas we think are most interesting. Sometimes we read the same materials together for even richer discussions. We know the rewards of reading and writing and then sharing together! When we share our responses to what we have read with others and listen to their ideas, we find that there are multiple layers of meaning—more than we constructed through our own interpretation of the text. The time spent discussing responses to the same text deepens that text and helps it take on new meanings. It is part of the joy and wonder of reading.

Our Beliefs About Learning

Read through the following statements and select the three that you think are most important and best reflect your priorities. Then get together with three other people and try to come to a consensus on three items that you all think are essential. Each team will then share their three items with the whole group.

_____ 1. Instruction in literacy needs to motivate students and be a pleasurable experience.

_____ 2. To invite students into reading, we need to find their areas of interest and provide materials they can read.

_____ 3. Many students, especially the boys, enjoy reading and learning about the real world.

_____ 4. Learning begins with questions. Until we experience some sense of disequilibrium or uncertainty, we are less likely to attend fully.

_____ 5. Students learn well from and with each other.

_____ 6. Elementary students should not spend much time reading nonfiction texts because they are not good examples of writing and are often boring in presentation.

_____ 7. Throughout life, most of us read more nonfiction (school reading and learning, news reading, pleasure reading, reading to be informed) than fiction. Teachers need to help students learn to become confident and strategic readers of these genres and formats.

_____ 8. Story is the most familiar form of literature to students; therefore, we want to build on that foundation and expand their experiences with increasingly rich pieces of fiction.

_____ 9. A good reading and literacy program balances fiction and nonfiction and teaches students strategies to be confident in reading each.

_____ 10. If students become interested, they will extend what is done in the classroom and engage independently and extensively. We need to help them find their questions and extend their curiosity.

_____ 11. Nonfiction reading workshops and mini lessons build a familiarity with these texts, so students can read them successfully.

_____ 12. Reading aloud to students means reading from a balance of fiction, nonfiction, and poetry that is generally more difficult than they would read independently.

Figure 1.4   Our Beliefs About Learning

Anticipation Guide:
Reading and Learning Priorities

Directions: Put an "A" before statements with which you agree. Put a "D" before statements with which you disagree.

_____ 1. Most students should know enough about reading by fifth grade that they don't need further help in developing strategies and skills.

_____ 2. Given content teachers' responsibilities, it is impossible to expect them to teach reading-thinking strategies.

_____ 3. Textbooks should be selected based on the depth and breadth of content material covered. The way ideas are organized in textbooks and the complexity of the writing are not nearly as important as the content itself.

_____ 4. Students should learn a small number of strategies and all teachers should help reinforce their use.

_____ 5. By the time students are in middle or junior high school, they should be independent learners and should not study in teams or cooperative groups. In life they will have to work alone.

_____ 6. Strategies for learning content material are different from those used in reading fiction either for analysis or for pleasure.

_____ 7. SQ3R (Survey, Question, Read, Recite & Review) is one of the best strategies to use when encouraging reading to learn even though it was developed in the 1940s.

_____ 8. Teaching students to summarize, make notes, and outline material should not be the responsibility of the reading teacher.

_____ 9. Students need more help with vocabulary because in content areas, terms convey and reflect important information.

_____ 10. Multiple texts help students think critically because they provide different points of view with differing content emphasis.

Figure 1.5   Anticipation Guide: Reading and Learning Priorities

Coming Together to Review Your Reading Program

Whole School Reading Audit

This tool is intended for use with school personnel and/or district or school improvement teams to

- reflect on current instructional reading literacy practices within the school,
- determine areas of strength and areas that need improvement, and
- guide the development of meaningful and prudent school improvement plans for moving a school forward in improving reading instruction and achievement.

This tool will generate the types of dialogue and staff development that will benefit the school in creating an understanding of its present reading program and developing plans to improve reading instruction for students. See Figure 1.6 for audit tool ratings and descriptions.

Audit questions are developed in six areas critical for quality reading programs. The areas include the following:

1. District/School Improvement Planning (see Figure 1.7)

2. Reading Curriculum/ Instruction (see Figure 1.8)

3. Reading Intervention (see Figure 1.9)

4. Staff Development in Reading (see Figure 1.10)

5. Assessment of Reading (see Figure 1.11)

6. Parent/Community Support for Reading (see Figure 1.12)

Evidence and Exhibits for the Reading Audit

The following may be used to demonstrate evidence:

1. Written evidence from school improvement plans and notes from meetings

2. Written evidence from curriculum meetings

3. Written evidence from school level meetings

4. Results of community surveys

5. Assessment results such as
   - achievement tests
   - state level tests
   - teacher and classroom assessments
   - local standards-based assessments

6. Curriculum guides

7. Results of staff surveys

8. Board meeting minutes

9. Samples of student work

10. Lesson plans

For the audit, a school may decide to complete the questions in all six areas or any combination of the six areas.

Illinois State Board of
Education Reading Audit Tool Rating

Rating	Meaning	Description
1	Weakness	Little or no evidence to indicate this area is a strength so therefore needs attention for improvement.
2	Acceptable	Reasonable evidence to indicate this area is a strength but could be improved with minor changes.
3	Good	Evidence suggests that this area is a district/school strength and contributes to positive student outcomes.
4	Exemplary	Strong evidence that this area is exemplary and contributes significantly to positive student outcomes.

Figure 1.6   Illinois State Board of Education Reading Audit Tool Rating

District/School Improvement Planning

Questions	Proof/Exhibit	Rating
1. Can staff members articulate the district's vision of reading instruction?		1——2——3——4
2. Are district goals established and is there a process for the communication and support of the district goals?		1——2——3——4
3. Do school improvement plans in reading/literacy align to district goals?		1——2——3——4
4. Has the district established grade level benchmarks indicating what students are expected to be able to do for each of the language arts standards?		1——2——3——4
5. Is a procedure in place for the establishment and maintenance of a district/ school improvement team?		1——2——3——4
6. How does the district/school improvement plan make reading/literacy goals and resources a priority?		1——2——3——4
7. What data does the district/ school improvement team collect to determine reading/literacy goals for the district/ school improvement plan?		1——2——3——4
8. In what ways does the staff assist and collaborate in the collection and analysis of data and contribute to an understanding of current results in reading/literacy?		1——2——3——4
9. How is collaborative leadership demonstrated to support reading as a priority by a. the faculty? b. the administration? c. the board of education?		1——2——3——4

Figure 1.7   District/School Improvement Planning

Reading Curriculum/Instruction

Questions	Proof/Exhibit	Rating
1. Do early childhood or kindergarten programs in your district incorporate literacy instruction?		1—2—3—4—N/A
2. Is reading instruction integrated with writing, listening, and speaking?		1—2—3—4—N/A
3. How do teachers model reading and writing processes and strategies for students?		1—2—3—4—N/A
4. How are opportunities provided to students to discuss material they read independently?		1—2—3—4—N/A
5. How do students participate in writing workshops?		1—2—3—4—N/A
6. How do teachers provide guidance on how to use classroom and school libraries?		1—2—3—4—N/A
7. How do students access classroom libraries?		1—2—3—4—N/A
8. How do students access the school library?		1—2—3—4—N/A
9. Do teachers read to students on a regular basis?		1—2—3—4—N/A
10. How much instructional time is devoted daily to reading/literacy? a. direct instruction of skills/strategies: b. guided reading: c. shared reading: d. reading aloud to students: e. writing: f. appropriate independent student reading: g. teacher reading conference with each student: h. teacher assessment of reading levels:	Weekly minutes: Weekly minutes: Weekly minutes: Weekly minutes: Weekly minutes: Weekly minutes: Weekly minutes: Weekly minutes: Weekly minutes:	1—2—3—4—N/A
11. How is instruction differentiated to meet the needs of all students?		1—2—3—4—N/A
12. How do teachers provide an emotionally safe environment for learning?		1—2—3—4—N/A

Figure 1.8

Reading Curriculum/Instruction

Questions	Proof/Exhibit	Rating
13. How are students grouped for reading? How flexible is the grouping plan?		1—2—3—4—N/A
14. How does the staff demonstrate high expectations for all students?		1—2—3—4—N/A
15. To what extent do all teachers view themselves as reading/writing teachers?		1—2—3—4—N/A
16. What suggests to a visitor that students are engaged in challenging and intellectual work?		1—2—3—4—N/A
17. How is each of the following topics addressed in the reading curriculum? a. phonemic awareness b. word study or phonics c. fluency d. vocabulary e. comprehension f. reading strategies for dealing with informational and visual text g. graphic organizers h. literary appreciation i. engaging students in reading j. metacognition k. writing		1—2—3—4—N/A
18. Do teachers have adequate instructional resources for teaching reading? a. leveled texts b. literature anthologies c. trade books d. word and vocabulary games e. newspapers f. magazines g. technological support or software		1—2—3—4—N/A
19. Is there evidence that reading and/or writing instruction is delivered in content areas other than language arts? a. reading b. writing		1—2—3—4—N/A

Figure 1.8 Reading Curriculum/Instruction

Reading Intervention

Questions	Proof/Exhibit	Rating
1. What early reading interventions does the district provide for students who demonstrate signs of difficulty learning to read?		1—2—3—4—N/A
2. How does the school ensure that interventions are integrated and coordinated with classroom instruction?		1—2—3—4—N/A
3. How is the effectiveness of the early intervention program measured in both the short and long term?		1—2—3—4—N/A
4. What training does staff involved with intervention receive?		1—2—3—4—N/A
5. What types of support services does the school provide students in Grades 3–12 who continue to struggle with reading?		1—2—3—4—N/A
6. How does communication occur regarding student progress a. between the reading teacher and the classroom teacher? b. between teachers within the same grade level? c. between teachers across grade levels? d. between the special education teacher and the classroom teacher? e. between the ESL teacher and the classroom teacher? f. between the teacher of the gifted and the classroom? g. between the parents and the classroom teacher?		1—2—3—4—N/A
7. What types of support services are provided to language minority students who struggle with reading?		1—2—3—4—N/A

Figure 1.9 Reading Intervention

Staff Development in Reading

Questions	Proof/Exhibit	Rating
1. How do the school improvement plans and professional development plans address reading instruction? Is there a clear connection?		1—2—3—4—N/A
2. What is the schoolwide plan for professional development in reading for the next 12 months?		1—2—3—4—N/A
3. Do teachers have access to sustained professional development activities?		1—2—3—4—N/A
4. How does the staff share knowledge, pool resources, provide peer support, and cooperate in learning from one another?		1—2—3—4—N/A
5. How do teachers obtain sufficient coaching for newly implemented instructional strategies?		1—2—3—4—N/A
6. Does staff have access to and utilize professional material in reading (e.g., magazines, books, and Web sites)?		1—2—3—4—N/A
7. What good practices have been put into place based on knowledge of current reading research?		1—2—3—4—N/A
8. How are new teachers mentored to teach reading?		1—2—3—4—N/A
9. How are paraprofessionals trained to assist classroom teachers in supporting reading instruction?		1—2—3—4—N/A
10. How does staff development increase student achievement?		1—2—3—4—N/A

Figure 1.10 Staff Development in Reading

Assessment of Reading

Questions	Proof/Exhibit	Rating
1. Are there district performance standards to guide reading instruction?		1—2—3—4—N/A
2. Is there alignment between district goals/standards and state goals/ standards?		1—2—3—4—N/A
3. How is student progress in reading measured and documented over time?		1—2—3—4—N/A
4. How is information from assessment used by staff to improve reading instruction?		1—2—3—4—N/A
5. What types of classroom-based assessment data are used to focus on students' individual needs and how?		1—2—3—4—N/A
6. Does program evaluation result in curriculum and instructional modifications?		1—2—3—4—N/A
7. How does disaggregated data influence decisions about improving the reading program?		1—2—3—4—N/A
8. How is assessment information passed on from year to year?		1—2—3—4—N/A

Figure 1.11 Assessment of Reading

Parent/Community Involvement

Questions	Proof/Exhibit	Rating
1. How are parents informed about student progress in reading?		1—2—3—4—N/A
2. How are parents encouraged to assist children in reading? a. Are workshops held for parents? b. Do teachers send weekly newsletters with reading tips? c. Are there incentive reading programs with sign-off sheets for parents?		1—2—3—4—N/A
3. How are parents and community members encouraged to participate in the school to promote student reading?		1—2—3—4—N/A
4. How are strategies to involve parents and community included in the district/school improvement plan?		1—2—3—4—N/A
5. How do district office personnel communicate with parents and community about reading?		1—2—3—4—N/A

Figure 1.12 Parent/Community Involvement

To Reflect

1. How do the ideas presented in Chapter 1 relate to your teaching experiences? What ideas support and confirm what you are already doing?

2. What did you find in this chapter that you can share with colleagues? Did something suggest new possibilities for your program?

3. What questions does this chapter raise for further discussion and reflection?

Coming Next

Teachers Working Together

Everyone Learns When Teachers Read Together

Shared Staff Study

Involve a Group in Local and State Professional Organizations

Create Structure for Professional Learning
> *Teachers as Readers Groups*
> *Professional Forums: Developing a Commitment and Plan*
> *Share Instruction With Video Clips*
> *Focus on Student Learning in Discussions*
> > Teacher Research

Coming Together in Reflective Teacher Groups
> *Specialists and Teachers Working Together*
> *Professional Literacy Networks*
> > The Whole Language Umbrella
> > Suburban Reading Specialists Network
> > Rutgers Literacy Curriculum Network
> > Reading Leadership Institute

Coming Together to Support Educational Reform and Change on the Consortium for Educational Change

School-University Partnerships

Coming Together in Cross-Institutional Partnerships: *The Emergent Reading Strategies Institute's Comprehensive Early Literacy Program*

Coming Together in Reflective Teacher Groups: *Everybody Reades Fluency Project. A Teacher Research Group Success Story Benefiting the Upper Levels*

Just Say "Yes"

To Reflect

● ● ●

Teachers Working Together

EVERYONE LEARNS
WHEN TEACHERS READ TOGETHER

As schools focus on improving student reading engagement and achievement, bringing together teachers and all others involved in instruction is important. Recent studies of schools that produce student learning well above that expected by their demographics identify teachers who engage together as learners as a key ingredient in their success (Center for Improving Early Reading Achievement [CIERA], 2001; Center on English Learning & Achievement [CELA], 2000; WestEd 2000). An analysis of the eight schools that won the Model Professional Development Award from the United States Office of Education found that these schools with teachers learning and working together had twice the student achievement gains of comparable schools, despite the level of poverty or transience. The report concluded that "At the heart of each school's success is an exemplary professional development program. . . . Teachers, paraprofessionals, and administrators have coalesced as learning communities and focused their own learning on what will translate into learning for students. Everyone is learning, and everyone benefits" (WestEd, 2000, p. 1).

Creating schools that hum with active learning and are real professional learning communities is challenging. However, there are many resources and professional groups available to support these efforts and increasing numbers of examples of schools that have reaped the rewards of

Getting the Most From Learning Communities

- Use clear, agreed-upon student achievement goals to focus and shape teacher learning.

- Provide an expanded array of professional development opportunities.

- Embed ongoing, informal learning into the school culture.

- Build a highly collaborative school environment where working together to solve problems and to learn from one another become cultural norms.

- Find and use the time to allow teacher learning to happen.

- Keep checking a broad range of student performance data.

(WestEd, 2000, p. 12)

their commitment. In this chapter many of these are examined. All involve some form of collaboration—either within a single school, as part of a larger network of teachers beyond the building level, or as a school-university partnership.

SHARED STAFF STUDY

One of the most natural ways for teachers to come together is to create a learning support team for themselves. A small group learning support team can expand so that shared instructional study becomes a part of the life of the school with staff time devoted to it. Committing to shared staff study is becoming more common. A culture where all teachers are valued and where questions and problems can be openly discussed is by necessity the cornerstone of successful shared learning. Establishing this level of openness and trust may take some time. Different approaches exist to address situations in which such a community has not been established or where it has become dormant.

In resistant settings, it may be easiest for two or three teachers who are interested in continuing their learning to simply make a commitment to each other to establish a regular meeting time together. The teachers select a topic that is of concern to all, and then each can select some articles to read and discuss together. An alternative format is for each teacher to bring in some samples of student work that are of concern and share these with the others in the group on a rotating basis. Getting the ideas and perspectives of other teachers on how to make the instructional activities more effective can be stimulating and, when done sensitively, can have lasting effects. With testing being such a dominant part of school life, finding issues and questions to study with a group is not difficult.

Some teachers have consciously taken time to belong to book clubs or literature circles to nurture their own reading and experience the same kinds of shared literacy that is the practice in their classrooms (Daniels, 2002). Talking in turn and staying on topic helps teachers understand the reality of literature discussion in their classrooms and helps them identify with students. Talking with students about particular experiences and insights gained in discussing a book with other adults helps make readily apparent one of the joys readers can have throughout life. Even when they are proficient readers, students are often surprised that adults respond differently to texts. Students can get very interested in their teachers' involvement in literacy and ask for stories from subsequent book club discussions.

The popularity of adult book clubs keeps expanding. Daniels (2002) reports that in many Chicago schools "we now work to develop simultaneous

---

Professional Organizations

Association for Supervision and Curriculum Development (ASCD)
   http://www.ascd.org/

International Council on Education for Teaching (ICET) http://www.nl.edu/icet

International Dyslexia Association http://www.interdys.org

International Reading Association (IRA) http://www.reading.org/

Learning Disabilities Association of America (LDA) http://www.ldanatl.org/

National Assessment of Educational Progress (NAEP)
   http://nces.ed.gov/nationsreportcard/

National Association for Bilingual Education (NABE) http://www.nabe.org/

National Council of Teachers of English (NCTE) http://www.ncte.org/

National Education Association (NEA) http://www.nea.org/

National Institute of Child Health and Human Development (NICHD)
   http://www.nichd.nih.gov/

National Middle School Association (NMSA) http://www.nmsa.org/

North Central Regional Educational Laboratory (NCREL) http://www.ncrel.org/

Teachers of English to Speakers of Other Languages (TESOL) http://www.tesol.org/

---

book clubs of teachers, parents and kids—sometimes having all these groups read the same book and come together for a festival of sharing" (p. 6).

INVOLVE A GROUP IN LOCAL AND STATE PROFESSIONAL ORGANIZATIONS

One easy way to help faculty see the value in continued professional development is to involve them in local or state-level professional organizations. For us to grow as professionals, we should be connected to the larger professional community. A goal of many schools is that every faculty member is a member of at least one professional organization. This ensures that

Passing On What's Out There

Have a fair of sorts, where publications, conferences, Web sites, and other resources of organizations are reviewed. This coupled with some small incentive (even paying part of the membership or purchasing a school subscription to the association's journals) can bolster the professional identification of the faculty.

there is a continuing inflow of new ideas and perspectives. Being a member of a professional organization is especially important when the faculty find time to hear reports from those who attend meetings and read the professional journals and share ideas from them.

If your school does not have an active professional identity, begin with some group activities. Make it a social outing to attend a meeting together, and then follow up with a discussion of the content of the speaker or workshop. If your faculty has not been involved, this is a good time to encourage them to become members of the professional organization. One of the benefits is that teachers will also receive mail and e-mail communication that will put them in touch with others who are active professionally. It can be a first step in developing awareness of what is available. You could have a fair, where publications, conferences, Web sites, and other resources of organizations are reviewed, and then provide incentives for teachers to join.

Getting Professional Study Groups Started

- Teachers as Readers Groups
- Professional Forums
- Share Instruction With Video Clips

Use professional organizations' Web sites to find out what is happening, such as what conferences are coming to your area.

CREATE STRUCTURE FOR PROFESSIONAL LEARNING

Professional development needs to be structured to be valuable. Both topics and format need careful planning. There are two basic thrusts for ongoing professional development. The first is to come together around a topic of interest and to meet for a specified period of time. The second is to establish an ongoing conversation among staff based around some framework. In some districts the process of establishing and revising local standards and curriculum provides an impetus for such study and reflection. Adoption of new materials in reading and language arts is another opportunity to bring teachers together to engage in some study and professional updating. Most schools have found that professional discussions, no matter what their purpose, need to follow some format for them to be productive. It is too easy for meetings and the conversations to lose their focus without there being structure.

Exploring a Topic

One way to structure the exploration of a topic to the best effect is to select one topic and ask teachers to brainstorm their ideas about that topic while a recorder takes notes. Then these ideas can be clustered and topics for the discussion developed around the clusters because they represent what teachers know and are interested in. Questions can be generated from these clusters, too, as the group thinks about their differences and areas of uncertainty. This is, in effect, using the KWL process (Know, Want to Know, Learn by activating what the group knows and setting questions to guide learning) for professional staff development; and it can work nicely if teachers share a moderate amount of knowledge about the topic.

A second way to foster discussion is to ask two to three of the teachers to prepare ahead of time to talk about the topic for the benefit of the group. This can be a way to recognize the knowledge and experience of some staff members who might not otherwise have a forum in which to share some of their efforts. Including some samples of assignments and student work products can make the focus even more engaging for skeptics and eager learners alike. After the perspectives of each participant have been presented, the rest of the group can be asked to comment, beginning with "What I liked about these ideas was _____." Follow up with "What I would like to hear more about is _____." With a structure like this for the group to follow, discussion comes more easily and is more focused.

Several strategies are available to help groups get started.

Teachers as Readers Groups

Many teachers enjoy the opportunity to meet together to discuss books they are reading. A model developed by the Association of American Publishers (Dillingofski, 1993) suggests that teachers, principals, librarians, district administrators, and parents meet regularly to read quality children's and adolescents' books and an optional professional book. The model they developed suggests that every semester the group of up to 10 participants selects at least four quality children's books and one professional book. The group should meet at least six times and have a site coordinator as well as a facilitator to guide the discussion. Books can be selected from the International Reading Association (IRA) Children's Choices or Teachers' Choices or from other annual recommended book lists. Participants in the group make a commitment to read the book prior to the discussion, or if they haven't read the book, then they don't orally participate but just listen during the group meeting.

The discussions flow from reading logs or journals that participants maintain as they respond while reading. These written records of their thoughts provide the basis for the discussions. Participants write their entries about their engagement with the book, commenting on connections they find with the book theme and events, questions that are raised for them by the book, and reflections they make while reading the book. These journal entries provide the starting point for each meeting. After sharing from journals, participants can extend on these ideas orally—and so the discussion evolves.

Professional Forums: Developing a Commitment and Plan

In recent years there have been many hot topics that have served to bring professionals together. Assessments, standards, reduced class size, elimination of reading specialists—the list goes on and on. You can capture these important issues by creating a professional forum for discussion and in-depth exploration of ideas. A way to begin dialogue is to bring teachers and administrators together and discuss ways they want to learn together. Working out some options is useful so there is not a lot of wasted time. Working from a set of ideas allows others to bounce off of them and create something shared even if the plan that evolves looks nothing like the original proposal. One group of teachers decided to combine reading articles, having some of the teachers share their work, and inviting a speaker from another local district to talk with them.

Structuring the Sharing of Video Clips

1. At each meeting, one teacher is responsible for bringing a videotape of him- or herself illustrating either something that worked well or a question or problem.

2. The group views the tape. No one is allowed to comment while the tape is showing.

3. After viewing the tape, each person, except for the teacher on the tape, tells what he or she liked on the tape.

4. Each viewer poses one question about the lesson.

5. The teacher on the tape is then given the floor to comment, both to describe aspects of the lesson and to respond to the questions.

Share Instruction With Video Clips

If teachers have a level of trust in one another, they can gain a great deal by sharing video clips of their instruction and use these as a point of discussion. Beginning with clips that the teachers are proud of is a way of introducing themselves to one another. Most teachers have no idea how others teach or handle the daily routines of keeping students on track and involving as many as possible in discussions of reading selections. The opportunity to visit other classrooms in this way can be very stimulating. It is hard to find a great classroom snippet, however, so the expectation should not be made too high for what is shared. One of my colleagues and former doctoral students developed a format for sharing based in videos, which works well for teachers (Passman, 1999). The structured format makes the teachers comfortable and willing to share. The results of this kind of focused professional development create an open and rich experience that has expanded to other groups and schools. To learn more, see the Coming Together on Reflective Teacher Practice Groups.

Focus on Student Learning in Discussions

Pat Carini, whose Prospect School was built on a model of teacher descriptive inquiry and shared reflection, has developed guidelines for teachers to engage professionally. Teachers use their own students as the starting point in their reflection of their work as professionals. They focus their teacher lens on the students and write weekly descriptive comments (three to five sentences in length) about each student. Weekly staff development meetings focus around the descriptive review of one student selected by the teacher who was doing the review that week. Teachers share student work samples, drawings, teacher observations, and weekly comments. For a more complete description of how to learn from student work, consult Himley and Carini's *From Another Angle: Children's Strengths and School Standards* (2000).

Teacher Research

Some schools find that teachers or some teachers prefer to engage in their own classroom research and only come together periodically. The Teachers as Researchers Movement has been popular in some areas, and there is a history and culture of teacher inquiry. If this is not the case in your school, it might be interesting to read the reports of some teacher inquiry projects and see if teachers might like to make a commitment to researching topics of interest. By jointly making a commitment to pursue key topics and questions through teacher research and inquiry, teachers can establish a shared support group to stimulate their deeper reflection and learning from one another.

Coming Together in Reflective Teacher Groups

Addressing the Human Aspects of Teaching—Building on the Reflective Practice Discussion Group

—*Roger Passman*

Reflective practice gets much theoretical play in professional development literature, including Berthoff (1987), Cole and Knowles (2000), and Lytle and Cochran-Smith (1992). Yet the sad fact is that little or nothing is done in schools or, for that matter, in colleges of education to provide either the time or resources for teachers to engage in meaningful reflection. In stark contrast to the norm, I have worked for the past several years with a number of teachers in various school districts, with full administrative support, to build a model for meaningful reflection growing out of the reflective conversation model developed and described by Carini (1986 & 2000). This model focuses teacher discourse on evidence of teaching practice. I call this focused, rule-governed discourse model the Reflective Practice Discussion Group (RPDG) (Passman, 1999).

To engage teachers in a reflective discussion about teaching and learning, some RPDG groups use self-created videotapes of participants teaching a lesson as a means for examining pedagogy in action. Other groups choose to focus on student-produced writing to focus their discussion on teaching and learning. The use of a particular teaching exhibit is dependent on the goals of the project. Videotapes are quite useful when the goal of the project is to generally affect teaching styles. When the goal of the project is, however, to have an impact on student performance, then using the student-created products or performances is a good choice. Either approach when matched with the goals and needs of the project can enhance the quality of the discourse.

Reflection Practice Discussion Group (RPDG) Rules

The rules are simple:

- Participants (1) examine the evidence of practice, (2) describe what they observed, and (3) raise questions and speculate about the artifact as the artifact-providing participant listens and takes notes in silence.

- The evidence provider then responds to the prior discussion, answering questions, addressing speculations, and commenting on what he or she found unexpected in the conversation while the other participants, in turn, listen silently.

- This is followed by a general discussion among all participants centered on what role the evidence plus the discussion plays in teaching and learning.

The RPDG engages teachers in a moderated discussion that, as far as possible, limits the expression of judgment or judgmental comments. Grounded in part on Habermas's (1979) early notions of communicative action and his description of the Ideal Speech Situation (ISS), the RPDG approximates an ISS by creating an environment in which participants engage in mutually beneficial discourse without feeling the need to stake their territorial claims through strategic action. The discussion is moderated. The moderator, generally a respected neutral party not participating in the group discussion, is charged with keeping the discourse on track and reminding participants of the rules. One of the participants supplies the artifacts of practice, either the self-created videotape or samples of his or her students' writing, used to focus the discussion. Each person gets a chance to present an exhibit. This allows each participant to contribute to the process. (See the Reflective Practice Discussion Group Rules sidebar.)

The RPDG is an ongoing process, lasting at least one academic year. A long-term commitment to this process is essential. Conversations at the beginning tend to focus on external problems of teaching, such as blaming the school board, administrators, and the "dreaded" test for the problems associated with teaching. By midyear, participants have begun to internalize their teaching, telling stories about their work. At the end of the school year, participants are engaged in a discourse of progressive change, focusing on their individual ability to support one another while, at the same time, focusing on engaging students. The discourse of blame is all but forgotten. This pattern is similar to that described by Knowles and Cole (1996), in which they identify three patterns of teacher development:

1. Strategic compliance, corresponding to early RPDG discourse, is a stage when teachers do no more than comply with demands.

2. Internalized adjustment, similar to midstage RPDG conversation, is evidenced by a change in thinking in response to systemic demands, but not necessarily a change in practice.

3. Strategic redefinition, paralleling the last phase of RPDG discourse, is evidenced when an individual redefines the dynamics and/or conditions for the context of systemic pressure—a transformation in practice.

Participating teachers value their experiences as members of an RPDG. Florence, a seventh grade social studies teacher, said, "I really didn't want to do it. I was frightened. I didn't want to make the commitment and I didn't want to be on video . . . but I was so glad I did it. It forced me to look at myself on video and I was pleasantly surprised." The idea of the vulnerability incumbent on self-taping her teaching nearly led Florence to not volunteer for the project. Her participation, however, led to an extraordinary change in her performance as a teacher.

Perry, a fifth and sixth grade bilingual teacher, said, "The [RPDG] is probably the single most, what can I say, creative experiences that I've had. It's creative because you look at what you're doing and it's examined by your peers . . . and because they're nonjudgmental in their valuation, you really get a good look at what you're doing." Perry found the self and group examinations to be creatively exciting. His analytic approach forced him to recognize changing practice through others before he saw change in himself.

Focused reflection gives special value and credence to teachers' voices in an authentic and productive way. Both teachers and their students benefit from the encounter.

Specialists and Teachers Working Together

One important way to increase professional conversations in a school is to rethink the relationship between classroom teachers and specialists. One model that is gaining popularity is to shift reading specialists from a focus only on instruction with special needs readers to having them function as coaches in the classroom, working directly with teachers to provide good instruction (Walpole & McKenna, 2004). This shift in role takes a great deal of preparation; yet when done carefully, it can be very beneficial to the district. The collaboration between classroom teachers and specialists or coaches encourages consideration of multiple perspectives and points of view in addressing student learning. It makes differentiation of instruction much more possible both in planning and in orchestrating activities.

Because it is clear that working together to improve reading for low-achieving students has positive results, it is worth the time spent in consideration of the emerging shared role of reading specialists and coaches.

As a result of a study (Ogle & Fogelberg, 2001) of reading specialists who were shifting their roles to work with middle grade classroom teachers more directly in classroom settings, nine conditions that support this new working relationship are included in Figure 2.1. The effectiveness of collaborations between classroom teachers and specialists has led to an increased reliance on such teaming of efforts. However, the changes required are significant and all teachers have to expend more effort in learning how to listen and respect each other's priorities and styles of working. Making such new forms of cooperation happen is challenging as well as rewarding.

Professional Literacy Networks

Often reading specialists, coaches, and teachers at a mature stage in their professional lives need to look beyond their own school for a professional development support network where people with similar interests can gather together for learning. One of the first large-scale networks was developed during the early years of whole language when teachers who were embracing whole language often found themselves as lone voices or at least in a minority in their schools.

The Whole Language Umbrella

Teachers from various other schools who shared their philosophical orientation came together to discuss their instructional concerns, eventually forming whole language study groups. The study groups were networked together quite soon into the Whole Language Umbrella, which became a large international network. The study groups served a very valuable function for teachers who wanted to share their ideas and celebrate their successes together. The groups were also a place where teachers kept learning. This network is a great example of what a group of committed teachers can do beyond the regular system. Many local groups still meet. Some have morphed into ongoing support groups, and some are now book discussion or writing groups. A national conference is still held each summer under the auspice of the National Council of Teachers of English (NCTE).

Suburban Reading Specialists Network

In Illinois, two reading specialists created a Suburban Reading Specialists Network to bring speakers to the Chicago area each year for professional development opportunities. The group meets twice a year for a luncheon and a speech by a prominent reading leader involved in a timely project. With little structure beyond the energy of Lynne Rauscher-Davoust, the luncheons have drawn from 200 to 500 people. Members network with other literacy leaders in the northern part of the state. An informal network for nearly 20 years until Rauscher-Davoust retired, a regional service center of the Illinois State Board of Education and an area reading council have continued the network.

Rutgers Literacy Curriculum Network

Dorothy Strickland, Samuel DeWitt Proctor Professor of Education at Rutgers University, began a network for curriculum directors and reading specialists several years ago. In the Rutgers Literacy Curriculum Network, Dorothy listened to the needs of school district leaders, invited speakers to address the members at monthly meetings, and then hosted the meetings and follow-up discussions. Network members had access to a variety of researchers speaking on topics of interest and were able to keep up-to-date in ways that would be impossible if they worked within their own districts. Individual districts didn't have the resources or the numbers of people

Nine Essential Conditions That Promote Effective Collaborations Between Reading Specialists and Classroom Teachers

1. Administrative Leadership

Principals need to be proactive in helping new partnerships evolve. Assigning students to classes, supporting choice in which teachers work together and how they work together, and providing incentives and resources are just a few of the ways effective administrators facilitate new arrangements.

2. Predictable Schedules and Routines

To make use of additional professionals in classrooms, there must be some regularity to schedules so agreed upon instructional arrangements can be realized. If special teachers end up sitting in a classroom watching the classroom teacher engage in whole-class instruction, the time is wasted.

3. Flexible Grouping in Classrooms

Added professionals need to be able to work with small groups of students. They can work most effectively in settings where students are comfortable in small flexible groups. When this is the pattern, adults can enter and not disrupt the whole class.

4. New Reading Curriculum, Textbook Adoption, and State Standards

Specialists find they can work easily with teachers as partners especially when there are new materials and curriculum to be tried. It levels the playing field and creates added reason for all teachers to rethink their instruction and be more open to variations.

5. Clear Operating Plan

Whenever two or more adults work together, having a clear set of processes and expectations makes life much easier for all involved. Since special teachers cannot be in the classroom all the time, these clear plans permit maximum productivity.

6. Choice in Teaming for Teachers

Because it is challenging for adults to work together, permitting some choice in initial teaming helps ease the changes. It is also true that some teachers never do well in shared settings, and these strong preferences need to be recognized.

7. Variations, Adaptations, and Flexibility

No one form of teaching or teaming works in all situations with all students. With the effort to provide instruction in the regular classroom, there are still times when both students and teachers recognize that taking students into a quieter and less stimulating environment may be most useful. Allowance for variation is crucial for both students and teachers.

8. Adequate Time Frame

Many students, and particularly struggling readers, often need longer blocks of time to engage in their reading activities. So, too, the change process requires time and effort. Therefore, being realistic and providing adequate time frames for both students' and teachers' learning is essential.

9. Open School Culture

For teaming and sharing of instruction to work successfully, teachers need to have an open attitude. School cultures either foster or hinder such sharing. The more the school is characterized as one where teachers learn together, experiment, and share their ideas, the more likely changing and new relationships and responsibilities will be successful.

Figure 2.1

SOURCE: Adapted from Donna Ogle and Ellen Fogelberg. Used with permission.

with interest at the deeper levels of the curriculum leaders. As part of the Network area leaders could meet with others in like roles and extend their knowledge and understanding.

Reading Leadership Institute

In the Chicago suburban area, Camille Blachowicz and I created the Reading Leadership Institute (RLI), a spin-off of Dorothy Strickland's idea.

However, because so many speakers come to the Chicago area, the institute's leaders (reading specialists, curriculum specialists, and interested teachers) wanted a format that permitted more discussion among them. Therefore, we have an evolving model that shifts each year. Our first year we surveyed the group to determine the issues they were facing in the schools. We finally focused on reading in Grades 3 to 5 since most districts felt it was an overlooked part of their literacy and general curriculum. We together developed a survey for the schools, and our members analyzed their own district programs and then shared the results with our group. From there we invited some speakers to talk with us and also began to do some writing about the needs at this level.

Coming Together to Support Educational Reform and Change on the Consortium for Educational Change

The Consortium for Educational Change (CEC) is a network of school districts and educational organizations that brings together teachers, administrators, staff, school board members, families, community members, and students. It is an organization that supports educational reform and change through collaboration among these various groups. Membership includes 50 school districts, the Illinois Education Association (IEA), Governor's State University, and National-Louis University (NLU).

CEC grew out of a school council in the Chicago area that, during the 1980s, included a group working on improving labor-management relations. This unique collaboration of members of both labor and management led to discussions about broader educational issues. Participants realized that such an approach could have similarly positive effects on other large-system changes in schools.

CEC provides member districts with a variety of activities to assist in effecting change. It holds quarterly forums, in panel or presentation format, on current reform topics. CEC sponsors an annual Summer Institute at which representatives from member districts discuss local change efforts and provide planning and sharing opportunities for collaboration. CEC also provides professional development programs for local districts through its emerging curriculum. Planners for this curriculum include representatives from the IEA and NLU, a local school board member, and a member-district administrator.

Activities sponsored by CEC are designed so that individuals with different roles in education and different "viewing lenses" can come together to discuss and plan effective change structures in schools. It is hoped that by approaching large-system changes as a team, these groups will have a better chance at long-term success.

Some of the activities of the RLI have included hosting an annual teacher renewal summer conference that summarizes the theme or topical issue studied that year, bringing in a few key speakers to dialogue with the group each year, meeting with our Illinois State Board of Education literacy leaders each fall, and writing a book grounded in the experiences of this group (Blachowicz & Ogle, 2001).

More forms of professional networks have been evolving over the last number of years, like the Reading Recovery Network and the Early Literacy Network out of Ohio State University. See Coming Together to Support Educational Reform and Change on the Consortium for Educational Change as an example of an area network supporting school change. These networks have developed as a way to bring together teachers and leaders who are engaged in developing a common model of literacy instruction. They hold conferences, have publications, and support the teachers in their networks in significant ways.

If you are not a part of a network and feel the need to reach out beyond your school, look for some group of like-minded and focused professionals and begin your own.

SCHOOL-UNIVERSITY PARTNERSHIPS

Many schools find creating and sustaining professional development difficult. It is often helpful to go outside the school and establish a partnership with some other agency or university. These partnerships usually develop when a school or district confronts a particular problem. Many times districts call on professional consultants to work with them on a limited basis. These relationships can develop into long-term partnerships. Productive and highly visible models exist, including those described by Osborne and Schulte (2001), Ogle and Fogelberg (2001), and Ogle and Hunter (2001). The impetus for some recent partnerships has been the need to find ways to include more special education students in the regular classroom. Other partnerships deal with the need to produce higher levels of literacy for all students with an increased focus on assessment and high-profile tests.

The Comprehensive Early Literacy Program described in the Coming Together feature evolved from collaboration between reading teachers in Arlington, Virginia, and faculty at the University of Maryland. The project is an example of an extensive collaboration for the improvement of literacy. This project, which lasted five years, began with a broad look at the foundations of literacy and the social contexts in which children become literate.

The Everybody Reads Fluency Project in the Coming Together feature is an example of how such projects develop from real school needs, how resources are found in a university faculty interested in pursuing such problems as developing literacy, and how both groups gain in the endeavor.

Coming Together in Cross-Institutional Partnerships

The Emergent Reading Strategies Institute's Comprehensive Early Literacy Program

—Janet Steiner O'Malley

John O'Flahavan, a faculty member from the University of Maryland and a researcher with the National Reading Research Center (NRRC), approached the Arlington, Virginia, Public Schools to join with him in an NRRC research project designed to develop a plan for transforming regular classroom instruction for low-achieving students. He was interested in taking some of the findings coming out of the Reading Recovery tutoring model and applying them to classroom instruction to try to accelerate the learning of low-achieving students. We have many schools with high numbers of culturally and linguistically diverse students, so the study had immediate appeal to many in the district, including myself. Because schools and classrooms are busy, complex places, the idea of linking to a university-based teacher-educator project seemed ideal as a way of sorting through the issues that affect kids and teachers. Therefore, I didn't have to think twice about saying "yes" and the same was true for the district. Arlington decided to accept this offer.

Included among the 30 participants were classroom teachers, Reading Recovery teachers, reading specialists, English as a Second Language (ESL) teachers, district literacy administrators, graduate students, and university professors. Within that group, 21 teachers came from four school sites. As we initiated our work together, we reflected on what we thought were the important components of literacy development. We investigated the principles of Reading Recovery (a one-to-one tutorial acceleration program for slow-progress grade one students) and studied the relationship between social contexts for instruction and students' literacy development.

We also set four broad goals:

1. Bring together the abilities of local and outside professionals.
2. Develop a framework for a comprehensive literacy program.
3. Evaluate the program.
4. Create a staff development model to suit the needs of teachers in our district.

Throughout the five-year project, the team came together in a variety of ways. Each summer our entire team worked in weeklong sessions to determine future directions and actions and to consolidate learning for the year. These back-to-back, full-day meetings accelerated what the team was able to accomplish. During the school year, the members also held monthly total team meetings. These meetings usually ran for two to three hours either after school or during school, with release time provided by the district. The monthly meetings helped sustain the focus on the theme: change.

The school-based teams met as often as each chose to support one another and to promote change within their respective buildings. In these meetings, we made a strong effort to get past the talk and into action. The teams problem solved, peer coached, modeled, brainstormed, and conducted workshops. The university-based researchers, who were former teachers for the most part, collaborated with us on new ideas and actions. The university researchers videotaped events, took field notes, and shared information with the participants between the monthly meetings.

District literacy administrators supported the work. They kept current with participants' change by attending team meetings. Through their efforts, the project received funding for summer sessions, increased release time during school, and additional student reading material in classrooms. Also, they supported a staff development model that evolved out of the project by providing funding for planning and instruction, textbooks, and recertification points for participants.

The team started our inquiry by looking closely at the principles of Reading Recovery to see how they might inform our regular classroom instruction. We talked a lot about the social nature of learning, videotaped instruction, analyzed our interactions, and learned to think differently along the way. The dynamic nature of inquiry proved fascinating. Once John tossed the first question into the water, its effect rippled on and on. One question generated many other questions, answers, and understandings. Those involved came to value what seemed like reaching a dead end because unexpected learning always came from having to change direction and action. Meaning developed from the feeling of chaos stimulated by John's strategy of always questioning the participants' assumptions and practices.

We also evolved innovative group contexts for students to socially construct their strategy use. This was an essential starting place without which analysis of individual practice and the understanding of how theory and practice relate could not have been realized. In time the team identified components of a supportive literacy environment, documented students' ongoing development, and analyzed the use of reading strategies by specific students. Then the team balanced the literacy environment by adding more components and evolved the Framework for a Comprehensive Early Literacy Program.

The components of the framework include

- continuous assessment of individual progress
- reading to, with, and by children
- writing to, with, and by children
- talking to, with, and by children
- activity centers for developing collaboration, independence, and autonomy
- embedded word studies
- home-school interfaces
- safety net interventions for students who fail to achieve on the school's schedule
- coordinated program and staff development structures

Each of the nine components features literacy in differing yet complementary ways.

A group of us Reading Recovery teachers developed and disseminated an emergent literacy framework to other teachers in the district. Among the outcomes of this effort was a movement throughout Arlington toward strategy-based instruction, word studies embedded in the language of the classroom, and instructional decision making that is grounded in developmental theory. To help deepen this understanding across the district, the team created a staff development course. The ongoing model, the Emergent Reading Strategies Institute (ERSI), offers 10 three-hour class sessions through which participants earn recertification credit upon completing course requirements. Admission to the institute is so popular that two simultaneous institutes were created to absorb the long waiting list. The course continues to evolve as more is learned both locally and from the larger professional community. In addition, ESL and upper-level and special education teachers have also asked to be included, which has helped shape the course. Some principals have also taken the course, and as they hire new teachers from within the district, they prefer those teachers who have been part of the ERSI course.

Everyone involved in the project gained a broader and deeper understanding of early literacy development. The Framework for a Comprehensive Early Literacy Program has been shared with other districts. By the end of our project, the participants understood that their design was relevant to upper-grade students as well.

The cross-institutional partnership allowed professionals to come together to bring about sustained and ongoing reflection and change in our instructional program. The university partners brought great perspective, which was invaluable to the success of the project.

Coming Together in Reflective Teacher Groups

Everybody Reads Fluency Project—A Teacher Research Group Success Story

The Everybody Reads Fluency Project grew from one school district's interest in readers at the low-middle achievement level—students who knew how to read but struggled with rate and accuracy. Faculty at NLU were interested in putting into practice in classrooms clinical findings about fluency instruction. The project was a collaboration between Evanston-Skokie School District 65 in Evanston, Illinois, and NLU to develop a group of teachers and community volunteers to improve reading instruction and reading achievement in the elementary schools.

Reading fluency is the ability to read at a good rate, with good accuracy, intonation, and phrasing. Research has shown that fluency is an accurate measure of overall reading performance and fluency practice in itself is effective in helping struggling readers improve their reading skills. In the first year, one teacher leader from each of thirteen schools and several NLU facilitators met monthly. They studied the research on fluency and developed instructional methods for building students' reading fluency. They learned a quick assessment method for creating a "fluency snapshot" of the class. Using this information, teachers planned and implemented reading activities involving both large and small group instruction.

That summer, a steering group of teachers made a handbook of ways for teachers to put a fluency spin on their language arts instruction.

The second year the project included an additional teacher from each school, a volunteer coordinator, and 50-plus community volunteer tutors. While teachers met monthly with facilitators to share activities, results, and ideas, volunteers were trained in repeated reading, a strategy to improve fluency. Volunteers were placed in teachers' classrooms, where they worked with four identified students twice a week. As students saw their reading rate and accuracy improve during each tutoring session, their motivation for reading increased dramatically. Pre- and post-assessments showed significant gains in students' fluency over the year.

After two years, teacher leaders and NLU faculty created handbooks and videotapes for ongoing staff development (see the Illinois State Board of Education Web site at http://www.illinoisreads.com/). Staff development and volunteer training continues, led by teacher leaders, the district literacy director, and a volunteer coordinator. More than seventy additional teachers and community volunteers have joined the project to learn strategies for improving students' reading skills through fluency practice. Subsequent work includes a book on how to implement fluency instruction (Moskel & Blachowicz, 2006) and a collection of research articles on fluency (Rasinski, Blachowicz, & Lems, 2006).

Benefiting the Upper Levels

Upper levels, middle and high school, also benefit from professional partnerships with universities. One good example is found in the Goals 2000 Professional Development Grant to the Chicago Public Schools (CPS). Deans from area universities met with the Division of Staff Development of the CPS at the beginning of this initiative and developed a model that involved each of the universities partnering with five city high schools to improve reading achievement. It focused on cross-curriculum involvement in literacy. The leadership team in each school, representing the major content areas, met each summer for three years with their university partners to develop their knowledge of the nature of active reading and specific content reading strategies that would help students achieve more in reading. During the school year the team became the leadership group for the school reading committees. The responsibility of the schools was to prioritize reading and have ongoing staff development activities at the school. One of the strengths of the model was that each of the participating high schools was connected to the university through a doctoral student intern who spent a day a week at the school. It was the intern who helped support the faculty of the high school in initiating changes in the classroom and departmental practices. The intern would often demonstrate teaching or coteaching with the faculty members, attend the reading meetings, and meet with the administration to further their commitment to the project.

The beginning of the project was difficult because there were huge differences in the knowledge and experiences of the teachers and university staff. Most high school teachers assumed that reading was for primary teachers and that reading equaled phonics and decoding. Yet by the second year there was a shared commitment to helping students become strategic readers and learners.

The school that showed the most significant gains (Ogle & Hunter. 2001) made reading their top priority for all students and had a strategy of the week that was the responsibility of all faculty to use in their instruction. The principal also used the strategies in his faculty meetings and required that student work be turned in with faculty lesson plans. Furthermore, the principal arranged for temporary assigned teachers and those needing help to attend Saturday staff development classes in reading offered at the school.

In each of the schools, there were common elements that led to their successes:

- Each school developed a shared commitment to content reading and made it a priority for all departments.
- Each school supported the development of new strategies on the part of the faculty.
- Each school created an infrastructure that could sustain their efforts.
- In two of the schools, the university interns continued to work as part of the school teams: one was hired as the reading specialist and another has continued as a consultant and now works for the central high school division. This partnership proved advantageous for the public schools and the university faculty and students in a variety of ways. It provided a context for the university faculty member to partner with administrators and teachers and test out ideas (Ogle, 2000) and provided a field site for doctoral students to also gain skills and conduct doctoral research (Boran, 1999). The schools gained by having an ongoing relationship with reading professionals willing to listen, and partner in dealing with real problems. (See Figure 1.10 in Chapter 1.)

Recently this university-school collaboration has continued through middle grade projects funded by the Chicago Schools. Both the Middle Level Project and the Mid-Tier Projects provided opportunities to work with particular schools to develop a team approach to literacy. In the Middle Level Project a small set of schools (8–12) were able to learn together and build a more substantial implementation of literacy across the curriculum. Each school developed a literacy team composed of representatives from each content area, special education, bilingual education and the library. The Lead Literacy Teachers (LLT) met monthly with Office of Literacy staff to learn about assessment and good instructional practices. The principals also had monthly meetings, some of which were combined with the LLT group. As a result of these efforts improvements in the schools were visible in improved reading scores, with some schools making substantial gains. This success and the efforts in developing differentiated content reading materials and strategies in the Mid-Tier Project were foundational in Chicago receiving one of the Striving Readers Grants from the U.S. Department of Education in 2006.

JUST SAY "YES"

Being aware of our own continuing participation in adult shared reading activities and groups, and sharing that with our students, helps keep fresh the ongoing roles reading can play in all our lives. Most adults read on the job regularly (Smith, 2000) for learning, for keeping up with our colleagues' activities, and for reinforcement. Helping students know about the benefits of being good readers is one of our responsibilities. We can do this in a variety of ways, only a few of which have been suggested here.

The enthusiasm engendered through cooperative relationships is aptly communicated by Janet Steiner O'Malley, whose district took part in the university-district partnership that developed the Comprehensive Early Literacy Program:

> If the opportunity comes your way, just say yes. Each of us has nagging questions about the decisions we must make in our classrooms; but we cannot easily get to the answers. Life there is fast paced and we have our minds on half a dozen things at the same time, and we are on our own. There seems to be a ceiling effect to how much we can learn if we keep to ourselves. That's why, at school when we need help, we go to a colleague who will lend us a perspective or an expertise that adds to our understanding; we need each other to learn and accomplish things. It's essential to be able to come together with others who share the same interest in the same questions with efforts structured for sustained learning to occur.

To Reflect

1. How do the ideas presented in Chapter 2 relate to your teaching experiences? What ideas support and confirm what you are already doing?

2. What did you find in this chapter that you can share with colleagues? Did something suggest new possibilities for your program?

3. What questions does this chapter raise for further discussion and reflection?

_____ **Coming Next** _____

Building a Literacy Community in the Classroom

Literacy Experiences and Backgrounds

A Place to Read: The Physical and Visible Environment of the Classroom
Making Students' Reading Visible in the Classroom
A Special Place for Students' Activities
The Author's and Reader's Chair
Reach for the Sky
The Role of Safety and Respect

Honoring the Individual in the Reader
Affective Engagement
The Older Student
KWL
The Power of Poetry
The Social Component of Learning
Book Clubs and Literature Circles
Partner Sharing
Think/Pair/Share
Partner Reading

Visual Engagement
Sketch to Stretch
Consolidating Ideas

Auditory Engagement
Student Oral Reading Forms
Dynamic Duo Reading
Radio Reading
Readers' Theater
Think-Alouds

Engaging Physically

Motivating Middle Grade Students to Read
Interesting Topics
Degree of Autonomy
Peer Interaction
Self-Efficacy

Conceptual Understanding
Teacher's Role in Ensuring Successful Experiences

Working With Other Adults in the Classroom

The Teacher as Reader

Coming Together to Learn From Each Other: Inclusion at Agassiz School

To Reflect

● ● ●

Building a Literacy Community in the Classroom

LITERARY EXPERIENCES AND BACKGROUNDS

Children enter our classrooms with very different literary experiences. Some come from families where reading is a regular part of their lives—parents who read to the children at night as part of a bedtime routine, who buy books for the children as special gifts, who visit the library and have their own personal collections of books and magazines. Others come from homes where there are no books, magazines, or newspapers. In fact, many children come from families who cannot read or do not read. Children also have very different personalities and preferences regarding how they engage in learning and in literacy. Some love to share ideas and talk with others about their reading. Some prefer to engage in a solitary way with their books and find writing in their own journals most satisfying. Others need to engage in dramatic presentation of characters or plays to feel they understand. Children vary also in their interests. Some prefer to read about the real world, and others love to enter imaginary settings and meet new characters.

Classrooms are also filled with students with very different experiences and levels of reading development. Our challenge in schools is to create a context in which all children come to appreciate and understand the important role literacy plays in our culture and can play in their lives. We want all students to value literacy as an essential part of their identity.

To make this a reality, teachers know that the basic goal is for students to develop the skills and strategies that enable them to easily and fluently read texts, stories, informational articles, songs, cartoons, and all matter of print. Teachers are the professionals who know how to develop students' reading.

We also know that those foundational skills and strategies need to be developed in meaningful and personally comfortable contexts. When students feel a personal purpose for an activity, they are much more likely to engage fully and persist until they have reached their goal. That means we, as teachers, need to get to know our students individually so we can invite them into learning on a personal basis. Some students will have had thousands of wonderful experiences being read to in their parents' laps during the first years of their lives. Others will have had no warm, personal book experiences at home. When inviting students into the joys of literacy, all deserve to feel the joys of reading as something that is shared with others close to them. These experiences can be built into classroom life if we make it a priority to insure our students develop not only the skills of reading but also the love of reading.

Students who connect personally with reading, who value reading and becoming literate, are much more likely to invest the energy, both cognitive and personal, in the learning and practicing that is essential for skilled reading to develop (Cunningham & Stanovich, 1998; Guthrie, Wigfield, & Von Secker, 2000).

The recent work that has been done on the role of affect in learning continues to underscore how important it is that we as teachers pay special attention to creating contexts where students feel valued and free to express their ideas, questions, and feelings (Goleman, 1995; Kessler, 2000; Noddings, 1992; Sylwester, 1994). What are some of the ways we can support students' development of purposes for reading in our classroom? As you think about this question you may recall some special events in your school years that excited you to become more of a reader. I know that my second and third grade teacher excited my interests in literacy as we engaged in extended units of study. We read about and learned poetry about the founding of the United States. I was Betsy Ross in the play we put on for our parents and the school where we recited, "Hats Off, the Flag Goes By" and other appropriate poems. I still have the portfolio of work that I did under Mrs. Keller's nurturing. Perhaps you can recall special teachers who instilled a love of language and reading in you.

I start this chapter by thinking broadly about the classroom contexts for reading development. In our age of testing and accountability, too many schools are rushing to the teaching of specific skills and outcomes. What we need are classrooms where students are motivated and encouraged to want to become readers. If we ignore this most basic aspect of our teaching, we will be less likely to find students who give their best efforts to the substantial learning that needs to be accomplished. A report by Essential Academic Learning Requirements (EARLs), a team of researchers from the University of Colorado who studied how the Washington state standards have been implemented, underscores this point well. As an example of how successful teachers weave together standards and engaging classrooms, the researchers (Simone, 2001) describe a specific fourth grade classroom where the teacher maintains her priority on meeting the needs of each student in a meaningful, student-focused learning environment. Students engage in regular class meetings where they work through academic and social problems, write purposeful and personal pieces during writing time, and gain the perspective of others with challenging problems as the teacher reads aloud to them from specifically chosen books. The author of the report concludes,

> To realize the potential of school reform, teachers must not only correlate the multiple dimensions of materials, pedagogy, curriculum, and their beliefs about teaching and learning, but they must also attend to the emotional needs of their students. School reform policy not only should aim to raise test scores, but also should encourage a change of heart about what it means to educate—to help students reach their potential. (Simone, 2001, p. 69).

In the midst of our rush to accountability and yearly testing of students' reading development, we must maintain our commitment to classrooms where students want to come and where they thrive under expert teacher guidance. Teachers have many ways they can create such classrooms. Students become readers when they are part of a community that invites them into the joys of literacy.

A PLACE TO READ: THE PHYSICAL AND VISIBLE ENVIRONMENT OF THE CLASSROOM

Immediately upon entering some classrooms you can tell that literacy is important. There is a reading corner with a table, bookshelves, and usually a rug and some comfortable chairs. Students and visitors feel invited to that corner—it is almost as if there is a magnet that draws you over to see what is displayed. Some primary classrooms use easels with books open and ready to be enjoyed. I walked into one primary classroom in New Zealand and had to duck because there were so many low-hanging little books held overhead by clothespins on clothesline rope. Books lined all the chalkboards. There were small bookcases everywhere. Even the students' desks, grouped together, had plastic bins of books in the center. Everywhere there were books! It was clear that this was a place where everyone read.

Other teachers find ways to display books by standing them on ledges and shelves, inviting readers to take and read. In middle school classrooms, teachers often use the vertical movable book racks that take little space yet display dozens of books. These also look like the racks in bookstores, so they build another level of association between classrooms and libraries and bookstores. Newspaper racks and magazine racks add a sense of invitation to readers of all ages. I enjoy visiting a middle school classroom where the teacher keeps the bulletin board near the door intriguing by posting a new joke or humorous story there every day. Sometimes she engages her students in puzzles and gives small prizes for the first student to figure out the puzzle. Teachers are creative in finding ways to display materials for reading; the key is to be sure that the priority on reading is visible and inviting to readers.

I have visited classrooms where teachers have made classrooms inviting in more idiosyncratic ways. One school's teacher had an old footed-bathtub in her room filled with pillows and a bookcase at the side. In another classroom the teacher had used a piece of play equipment that was constructed into a tree house-like reading room that students had to climb into. How they loved it! The space seemed private and special—made just for times to escape into books. Classrooms take on a real special character when there is a reading nook, a carpeted area or pieces of carpet that students can lie on, or old sofas and rocking chairs in corners where students can curl up and lose themselves in their reading. These unusual additions to the room certainly draw everyone's attention to them and make students more self-conscious about being engaged in reading as a social activity. To read is to do something special in a special place that is shared by the class.

Making Students' Reading Visible in the Classroom

Classrooms have wonderful spaces to show off students' responses to what they read. Bulletin boards are easily used to reflect students' engagement with literacy. Think of all the ways student work can invite others to read favorite stories and books about favorite topics:

- A bulletin board with students' drawings illustrating what they thought was most important in a book or in each chapter of the book being read by the class (*Stone Soup* at the primary level and *Bridge to Terabithia* at the intermediate level are examples.)

- A map students have created showing the spatial layout of the setting of the story, "The Iditarod"

- A full three-section bulletin board across the back of the room with a KWL (what I Know, Want to know, Learned and still need to learn) chart on the study of birds. (In one class, as students read more about birds, they made cards and drew pictures to illustrate what they were learning and posted them on the appropriate place on the board. Over a period of three weeks the knowledge students gained was visibly displayed for all to see.)

• An author study with pictures of the author and covers of the author's books interspersed with students' drawings and testimonials (Tomie de Paolo's many books would be an example).

Making Literacy Visible

Students can become book reviewers and print out their reviews on a special board.

Students can be in charge of keeping a news section of a bulletin board current.

Students can advertise new books that are noted in the Sunday newspapers in the children's book review section (many newspapers now include such a section) and in children's magazines.

Students can write their own reviews and post them on the walls along with reviews from children's magazines.

Students can identify parts of local newspapers that relate to literacy events. For example, many daily newspapers even have photographs of the authors who will be in the city during the week for book signings and speeches. Students can highlight such events and enjoy and begin to realize the active nature of literacy!

Even posting local events that relate to books and authors can make more real and tangible to students the ways literacy surrounds them.

Teachers who prioritize making literacy a visible part of the classroom keep thinking of new ways to realize this intent. (See the box above for tips for making literacy visible.)

A Special Place for Students' Activities

The classroom should also be a place where students' own book selections are honored. Is there a place where their books are kept for individual reading? In one primary classroom I know, there are plastic crates on the center of the table where the books are kept. Students have made their own bookmarks, which are kept in whatever book they are currently reading to mark their place and to help keep the "ownership" clear. The teacher also has a chart on the wall where students record each book they have finished and rate it according to a scale they have developed. Further reviews of the books are kept on a computer file so students can check out why someone really did like a book or did not.

The news that students want to share can also be taken from the local papers or student news magazines (*US Kids*, *Time for Kids*, *Weekly Reader*, etc.), and special stories can be featured.

The Author's and Reader's Chair

Many teachers have followed Don Graves's idea of having an author's chair in the room (Graves & Hansen, 1983). This can serve a dual purpose: It can also be the reader's chair. Giving students a special time to read from sections of their current reading choices brings a more central focus to the engaged nature of reading and makes it more shared and social. The chair itself reminds everyone that there is a time to share reading favorites.

Reach for the Sky

The ceiling and mobiles hanging down into the room can serve as additional locations of student work. Students can always see books, and the visual covers are enticements to read. In one intermediate classroom, students make mobiles of their favorite books and highlight aspects of the characters or events with real artifacts.

The Role of Safety and Respect

A key to creating classrooms where students are willing to share their own ideas and their engagements with what they read is making the classroom safe and making it one where all students feel respected. This is not always easy to do, especially where there are many cultural groups represented or where students tend to form cliques. Oldfather and Dahl (1994) developed a framework that can be used to assess the way classrooms respect students (see Figure 3.1).

HONORING THE INDIVIDUAL IN THE READER

As we create classroom cultures where students are respected and have multiple opportunities to develop intrapersonally and interpersonally, we know that there are variations among our students' learning. Educational research has suggested for some time that we learn in a variety of ways, including through emotion, image, sound, and movement. In reading, the dual coding theory of Sadoski and Paivio (2001) has extended the schema theory research to show that readers code information both linguistically and through nonverbal, mostly visual, processing. Gardner's work (2006) has highlighted the reality of Multiple Intelligences (MI) and differences in how we learn best. The accumulating work on MI challenges us to think

DOMAIN: CLASSROOM

Honored Voice: Condition of deep responsiveness in the classroom environment to students' oral, written, and artistic self-expression.

Sharing the Ownership of Knowing: Within the classroom community, the authority of knowing is shared by teachers and students through discourse patterns in which they collaboratively construct meaning in responsive and respectful ways.

Generative Literacy Curriculum: The meaning-centered literacy curriculum engenders and supports a "rich broth of meaning."

Supportive Social Structure: The social context for learning shifts as learners make various choices. Learners work in a variety of informal combinations that change from moment to moment.

DOMAIN: INTERPERSONAL

Constructing Meaning: Students engage with the literacy curriculum through processes of discovering and generating meaning and sharing that meaning with others.

Self-Expression: Through literacy activities students declare who they are, what they know, and what they care about. Their personal responses and individual voices are integral to learning processes.

Learning From Others: Learners exchange ideas and provide scaffolding for one another's work. The teacher functions as a learner in these exchanges and provides scaffolding for further learning.

DOMAIN: INTRAPERSONAL

Competence: Learners perceive a sense of competence as literate persons—as readers and writers who use tools of literacy for their learning goals.

Self-Determination: Learners perceive that they participate in shaping their learning agenda and that they have voice and choice about a variety of aspects of their learning within the given parameters of the curriculum.

Personal and Social Visibility: The literate community serves as a mirror that enhances the learner's sense of self as a valued participant in classroom discourse.

Epistemological Empowerment: Learners experience a sense of intellectual agency and ability to know that emerge from a sense of integrity of the learner's own processes of constructing meaning.

Figure 3.1

SOURCE: Adapted from "Toward a Social Constructivist Reconceptualization of Intrinsic Motivation for Literacy Learning" by P. Oldfather and K. Dahl in the *Journal of Reading Behavior.* © 1994

more deeply about both the nature of intelligence and the kinds of learning opportunities we provide our students. The more broadly we conceive our instructional options, the more likely we will meet the strengths of our students.

As teachers, we find it much easier to develop set routines and build instruction that fits our own habits and preferences rather than prepare instructional activities that meet the range of the intellectual strengths and preferences of our students. For example, I know some teachers who build literacy around students' individual work; they prefer not to have discussion groups and instead rely on student journals to develop engaged responses to literature. Other teachers need to work with groups and like to hear their students talk, overlooking the more private forms of response to reading. Few teachers seem to prefer the more dramatic, musical and bodily responses many students prefer. Gardner reminds us that almost any topic can be learned in a variety of ways. Therefore, as we create our classroom reading activities, we need to think carefully about ways we can involve more of the intelligences our students possess. We need to stretch ourselves and our students in new directions (Ogle, 1999).

AFFECTIVE ENGAGEMENT

Knowing our students means knowing their strengths as learners, their interests, their sense of themselves as readers, and their motivation and perseverance. It also means knowing who they hold as role models and what kinds of rewards for accomplishment are significant for them. Therefore, we need to be sensitive to the great range of student interest, preference, and ability in any one classroom and make our programs work for them.

Teachers are very creative and find unusual ways to make reading a shared and fun event. Yet we also need to listen carefully to our students and find what interests them and build those interests into our classroom activities and into the kinds of reading materials we promote. As we listen, it is good to make notes of things students talk about, what they bring to class to share or read, and how they spend their time. In doing so we are unlikely to overlook particularly good opportunities to make reading come to life for our students. It is also good early in the year to do a survey of students' interests, both in general activities and also in reading. There are many good student surveys available in print form, and they are easy to create. See Figure 3.2 for an example of a survey that can be used with older students. It can be readily modified to accommodate the needs of primary students. One of the best ways of determining students' interests is to listen to them. Ask them questions about what they do outside of school and make notes about what excites them. Then you can also determine interests if you do regular book and magazine talks for the students where you introduce several new selections and explain why you think they are good. Give students opportunities to sign up for their favorites and you can begin to watch patterns of interest emerge. Rather than the teacher doing all the work to determine some good interest areas, involve students too by having them interview one another so the class as a whole can start identifying topics and genre that are appealing. These can be included on a chart that is visible in the class so students can add to it as they find an author or genre or topic they are interested in sharing with others. This makes for a good starting place for finding material they would be interested in reading. Some teachers do talks on a variety of books and let students select the books to read. This is another easy way to start identifying preferences for books.

All students like to be included in classroom reading events, so be sure there is a variety of materials and a variety of reading levels in what is selected. We want students to feel successful in all they read, so having appropriate materials is important. Guthrie and Wigfield (2000) elaborate on the conditions that make for real engaged reading. They include

- clear purposes for reading,
- interest in the topic,
- comprehension of the material,
- confidence in one's ability,
- social interaction around the reading, and
- motivation to participate.

When reading is effective, many of these factors work together to influence the others. A key to motivation and engagement for all students is confidence that one can succeed and accomplish the task. Therefore, we need to be careful that we encourage students with reading that is within their range of possibility or that we scaffold the reading so they can be successful with some additional help.

The Older Student

As students get older, they become very conscious of what they can do. Very short, graphically attractive reading materials work as well for older students as they do for younger students. Identifying their favorite areas—whether a particular sport, fashion, movies, music, or personality—can make the difference in inviting them into reading or leaving them still holding the covers of the books and magazines shut.

STUDENT INTEREST INVENTORY FOR OLDER STUDENTS

1. What are the best things you have read? (Sports scores, music lyrics, magazines, books—you name it!)

2. What kind of material would you most like to read if you had time? What author would you choose to read?

3. What's the best book someone has read aloud to/with you? Why did you like it so much?

4. Have you ever read a book and then seen the movie based on that book? Which did you like better and why? (like Harry Potter, for example)

5. What are you most likely to read if you have a newspaper? (Show a student a newspaper if you can or use the local newspaper.)

6. Which of these magazines would you most likely read? (Show 4–5 magazines—for example: *Cobblestone*, *Sports Illustrated for Kids*, *Ebony*, *Time for Kids*, *National Geographic World*, *Science*, or some other specific content issues or popular movie and music magazines.)

7. Do you like history, biography, fantasy, or science fiction? Can you think of a good example of one of these books that you like?

8. What do you like to do with your free time after school?

9. What would you like to learn about or learn how to do?

10. How do you choose materials to read when you can decide for yourself?

Figure 3.2   Student Interest Inventory for Older Students

KWL Worksheet

1 What We Know	What We Want to Learn	What We Learned and Still Need to Learn

2 Categories of Information We Expect to Use	3 Where We Will Find Information
A.	1.
B.	2.
C.	3.
D.	4.

Figure 3.3

Kindergarten KWL

Dear Parents,

The Kindergarten children have been studying animals. As part of our animal study, the children have completed the first two steps of our KWL.

First, we listed all the facts that we KNOW about animals and individually illustrated one fact.

Second, we listed all of the things we WANT to learn about animals. Now, we plan to complete our KWL. Your child has chosen one question to answer. Please follow the directions below and complete the assignment with your child.

Directions for KWL	Question:
1. Discuss the question.	**I learned that:**
2. Discuss with your child ways in which you could complete your research.	
3. Research together.	
4. Once you find the answer, discuss your answer together.	
5. Have your child retell the answer in his or her words.	
6. Print your child's response, or, if your child prefers, he or she may "write" the response.	
7. Have your child illustrate his or her answer.	
Return it to school at your earliest convenience.	
Thank you.	
The Kindergarten Teachers	Name_____

Figure 3.4

SOURCE: Used with permission of Debbie Gurvitz.

KWL

Honoring what students know is another important way of effectively engaging students. Using a KWL framework (see Figure 3.3; see Figure 3.4 for a sample KWL activity) for informational reading allows students to think about their own relationship to the materials—what they Know (K), what they Want (W) to learn, and ultimately what they did Learn (L)— which places the student at the center of his or her own learning. KWL is widely used by teachers as a way of building on students' interests and knowledge when studying informational topics. The teacher guides students in brainstorming what they already know about the topic and elicits their questions both at points of disagreement and later when their knowledge has been shared. The teacher serves as scribe and records on the board, transparency, or large sheet of paper what the students volunteer without editing or correcting their ideas. As part of the initial phase of activating what is already known, the teacher also leads students into thinking about how the topic is likely to be organized by asking, "What categories of information do we expect on this topic?" These are listed under the Know column and can serve as an entry into questions. For instance, as students are brainstorming what they know about penguins and come to the listing of categories, they suggest that habitat, varieties, enemies, life cycle, family, and relation to humans are likely. Then they revisit the list of what they brainstormed and note that there is nothing about enemies or life cycle listed. This then leads to questions for the Want to know column and the beginning of some real inquiry on the part of the students. The teacher writes down the class contributions and then asks students to individually create their own KWL charts that they will use to record what they learn. With this step completed, the students turn to their resources and make notes in the Learned column as they encounter new information or find confirmation of points that were contested by the class. The third column (Learned/Still need to Learn) is where students write what they learned and also what they realize they still need to learn to serve as a guide for ongoing thinking. The more students take ownership of their own study, the more they realize the depths that are possible for them to continue building their understanding. This open-ended extended attention to topics by students is one of the major advantages of using the KWL process. Students begin to realize that learning is natural and fun!

Since the introduction of KWL, teachers have found many variations on how to use it (Rasinski & Padak, 2000). The first major shift occurred when teachers found it could be used very well for units of study that went beyond a single textbook. We added a section on the chart to include How/Where I will read (Ogle, 1989) to reflect this shift. Then Hoffman

(1992) developed the I-Chart (see Figure 3.5), which extended the KWL so students who wanted to go more in-depth in studying a topic could do so easily. The I-Chart grid has columns in which students list three focused questions and also has rows for three to four sources of information. Students search each source to see how the authors answer their questions. The final column is for students to synthesize the information and summarize an answer to each of their questions.

Primary teachers have used their bulletin boards to create open-ended spaces for students to engage in an ongoing learning process. One section of board is used for each part of the KWL. As students read many sources and find answers to their questions or new information that is interesting to them, they write the information on index cards or strips of paper. These are tacked to the board either beside the question or in the Learned column. New questions are added on colored strips of paper as students ask them. If students locate information that modifies what they thought they knew, they learn to use editing marks to change their statements. They may use a caret to add or limit statements and cross out parts that are erroneous (and give the source they are crediting for changing their ideas).

Another important addition to the KWL was developed for older students who need to remember information they learn from their reading. KWL+ (Carr & Ogle, 1987; Ogle, 2006) provides added steps so students process information more thoroughly and make it their own (see Figure 3.6). Using the "+" of KWL, students take the information they knew before studying, combine it with what they learned, and create a graphic organizer of all this knowledge. The categories they generated before reading may be used, or those may be altered based on the reading and learning. Using their graphic organizers, the students then write a summary of the content. By transforming the information and concepts into both a graphic and verbal form, students process the ideas more deeply and are more likely to remember them. One study using KWL+ (Jennings, 1991) showed that when students summarized by writing a journal entry from a personal perspective, their retention was even higher.

Teachers have also found that KWL and KWL+ can be used to help evaluate students' learning of process and content. By keeping copies of student KWL charts over time, teachers and students can see the evolution of students' engagement. Their questions should improve, their categories become more appropriate, and their linking of knowledge to what they asked should be clearer. One Title I teacher (McAllister, 1994) developed a group record-keeping format so she could tally each time a student contributed to any of the three parts of the process. She also made notes of the quality of their contributions and used this as a way of ensuring the students were learning to participate in the process individually, and she shared these records with the classroom teachers.

I-CHART

Topic	What We Know	Source 1	Source 2	Source 3	Summary
Interestig Facts					
New Questions					

Guiding Questions

Figure 3.5

SOURCE: Adapted from Jim Hoffman (1992). Copyright 1992 by Jim Hoffman. Used by author's permission.

KWL+

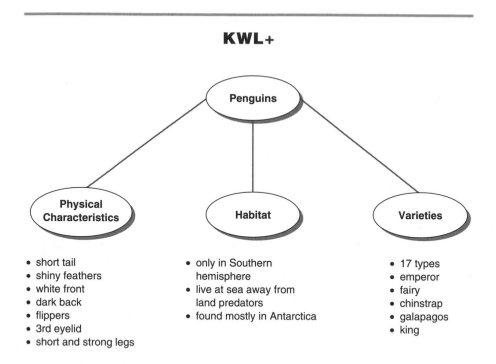

Physical Characteristics
- short tail
- shiny feathers
- white front
- dark back
- flippers
- 3rd eyelid
- short and strong legs

Habitat
- only in Southern hemisphere
- live at sea away from land predators
- found mostly in Antarctica

Varieties
- 17 types
- emperor
- fairy
- chinstrap
- galapagos
- king

Penguins are very special birds. They are warm blooded and lay eggs. They have short tails, a lot of shiny feathers covering their bodies. Their feet are short and very strong. They have white fronts and dark backs.

All Penguins live south of the equator. They live at sea but some go on land to lay eggs. Most Penguins are found in Antarctica where it is very cold. But Some Penguins live near where it is cold. But, some penguins live near where it is not.

The chinstrap penguin is the most common. There are 17 different kinds of penguins. Emperor penguins are the biggest. Fairy penguins are the smallest penguins. Other penguins are King and Galapagos.

Figure 3.6

Finally, some teachers have used KWL as a framework to involve parents and family members in class study themes. Gurvitz (1999) begins her monthly kindergarten units by involving students in brainstorming what they know and then helping them frame questions. Working with the school learning center director, Gurvitz is able to collect materials students can access in the classroom. The class also spends time in the learning center learning how to locate and use print and electronic resources. As they begin their inquiry, each student then selects one of the questions to take home (on a special Home Link form prepared by the teacher) and research with family members. What is learned is then drawn by the student—parents may write some elaborations—and returned. All these sheets are displayed on the class bulletin board, and students share orally what they learned with their classmates.

THE POWER OF POETRY

Reading and responding to poetry are great ways to address the affective element of learning. Cinquains, acrostics, and phrase poems are especially good forms for eliciting personal connections, feelings, and images. Cinquains are five-line poems that follow a special format. The first line is the one-word topic, the second line is two adjectives that describe the topic, the third line has three *-ing* words that describe action, the fourth is a four-word phrase that describes a feeling about the topic, and the fifth concludes the poem with a one-word synonym. Here is an example using the word *books*:

Books

Personal, profound,

Probing, stimulating, comforting

Companions on life's journey

Friends

Acrostics are created by taking the letters of the theme word, placing each in a vertical line, and then creating lines for the poem using each letter. Here's one on books again:

Best friends

Opening new worlds

Orchestrating my adventures

Keeping records of past and current memories

Special, every one!

Shape poems are also fun—the poet writes the lines of the poem in the shape of the content. For example, if the poem is about a sailboat, then the lines are written to create that shape; or if the theme is baseball, then the shape might be either of a ball or a bat.

THE SOCIAL COMPONENT OF LEARNING

Many children become readers because their friends are readers. Even if they don't see parents or other adults reading much, shared fun from reading that occurs in the classroom can make a tremendous difference in students' interest and engagement in literacy. There are several ways we can build these shared events in our classrooms.

Book Clubs and Literature Circles

Recent interest in developing students' abilities to share their responses to reading has led to a variety of structures that facilitate talk about books. A key to these literature discussions is that they are student led and generally involve from four to eight students. The groups may be transitory, just for the reading of a single book, or more sustained (Calkins, 2001). Teachers' roles in these small groups are as facilitators and observers rather than as the leaders. As discussed in Chapter 2, many teachers have been using some form of book club (Raphael & McMahon, 1994) or literature circles (Daniels, 2002). These formats for students to read and discuss books they read together encourage great sharing of ideas and feelings. Teachers who decide to use some sort of book club or literature circle make them the central structure for their reading instruction.

Partner Sharing

It is also possible to encourage sharing without using more elaborate formats. We have found that a good beginning step most teachers can use is having partner responding included periodically as part of instruction. Even in kindergarten and primary classes when teachers have children on the carpet and read to them, they can stop periodically and ask students to turn to the student next to them and respond—maybe telling what they predict will happen next, which character they like better and why, or what they would do in the same situation. Teachers who have learned some of the cooperative group strategies (Johnson & Johnson, 1990) instruct students to use their 12-inch voices or their knee-to-knee voices. Any oral mode of communication is likely to need some teacher guidance before students know how to use it comfortably, but the instruction pays off well when students become thinkers and sharers together.

One of the easiest ways to help students learn to share ideas is to simply pair up class members; students can select their own partner or you as a teacher can assign them. You may have students change their partners periodically so different voices are heard together. As the class is reading a particular text, either in literature or in informational material, provide some stopping points where students can discuss the ideas with their partners.

Think/Pair/Share

One format for partner sharing, developed by McTighe and Lyman (1988), is called Think/Pair/Share. In this simple format the teacher poses a question and has students individually write their own answer to the question. Then the teacher has students pair up and share their answers with their partners.

Discussion Starters

I predict. . .
I feel. . .
I connect. . .
I wonder. . .
I don't understand. . .

Figure 3.7

Finally, after the partners talk together and clarify their ideas, the whole class reconvenes and ideas are shared generally. Using this format we find that students gain more confidence in their own ideas when their partners validate them. They also may be pushed by their partner to clarify what they mean and as a result may modify their answers before having to expose them to the whole class.

Many students, and perhaps especially English as a Second Language (ESL) learners, are much more comfortable talking about ideas when they can do it one-on-one rather than in a whole group. The teachers gain insights into the students' thinking by listening in as the partners talk. One teacher found that her students were more comfortable when they didn't return and share in the whole group but let the teacher summarize and clarify their ideas gleaned from listening to the partners. This teacher kept changing the partners too, so the students learned to listen to one another and gained respect for others' ideas.

Creating ongoing partnerships so students gain comfort in working together can enhance sharing too. Teachers who pair students as classroom reading buddies create the conditions in which students can learn to

SIMPLE SYMBOLS FOR MARGIN NOTATIONS

!	=	a new insight or interesting point
+	=	something important to be remembered
?	=	something unclear that I want to go back and discuss
–	=	something I disagree with
✓	=	confirms what I already knew

Figure 3.8

talk about what they read. In reading buddies programs the teacher and class generally decide on a certain amount of text to be read. Then the reading buddies meet and discuss their responses. A guideline for the kinds of responses that are appropriate helps build students' understanding of how to talk with others about their reading. A bookmark that includes good discussion starters for reading buddies is shown in Figure 3.7. As students proceed through books together, their discussions become deeper and more interesting. This shared meaning develops in ways that are not possible in large group discussion.

Partner Reading

Some students do better when they combine oral reading of a text with discussion afterward. In partner reading the text is divided into short segments. Both partners silently read their segment making sure they know the words and can read it fluently. Then the first reader reads his or her segment orally while the other listens. We have used two formats for partners talking and thinking about the text as they read together. The first is to have the listener summarize the ideas in the text and ask questions if clarification is needed. After this reflection, the second reader reads his or her portion orally, and the other partner listens and then summarizes and clarifies. The reading proceeds this way with turn-taking until the determined amount of text is completed. The second format we have used is to have both of the partners write a question or two they will ask the listener when their oral reading of each page is completed. The listener does not initiate the questions or summary—the reader of that portion of the text does. (See Text Set Guides for CPS Mid-Tier Project for examples of how this functions.)

VISUAL ENGAGEMENT

Much of what we learn is stored visually as well as in verbal forms. The research of Sadoski and Paivio (2001) on dual coding and other instructional studies have confirmed the importance of visualizing in reading. Long, Winograd, and Bridge (1989) found that fifth graders experienced imagery spontaneously and consistently. Gambrell and Bales (1986), working with young readers, found that training them in visualizing while reading enhanced comprehension and memory. Pressley et al. (n. d.) also identified visualizing as one of the key strategies of proficient readers. Recently, Zeigler and Johns (2004) compiled a good resource on visualization strategies that includes many ideas for strengthening students' visualizing as does Ogle's (2000) focus on making reading more visual. A few key suggestions for utilizing students' visual strengths are included in this section. Think of ways you help increase your students' activation of their visual tools.

Students can create visual images that help them connect nonverbally with the material. This can be done before, during, or after reading. Visualizing images while reading can be effectively used with fiction and nonfiction material by having students draw images after each paragraph or chapter.

Making notes in the margin of books is a simple and effective way to directly engage with the text. Using a simple set of symbols, such as those shown in Figure 3.8, students can respond to the text as they read. Readers can note the appropriate symbol in the margin. Another method, one that doesn't require writing directly in a book, is using sticky notes or bookmarks. Students can also use sticky notes to comment on something in the text with the added benefit of being able to remove their notes and compare them with a partner or in small groups. Other useful tools are bookmarks, like the one shown in Figure 3.7, or strips of paper on which the student writes key words or predictions related to the text.

Sketch to Stretch

Short, Harste, and Burke (1996) developed the strategy Sketch to Stretch, which has students draw the central idea of the text they have read and then share these drawings in a small group. When they gather, each person takes a turn and shows the small group his or her drawing. Then group members orally express what they see in the drawing, with the artist-reader taking the final turn to explain the reason behind the drawing. If the groups want to, they can select one of the drawings to share with the whole class later. In this way there is a nice combination of visual response with verbal response. Students talk about someone else's drawing before they have to express their ideas and feelings about their own drawing, which can make the sharing easier. It is also interesting that this form of sharing involves many students who otherwise are often left out of the verbal discussions that go on around literature.

In his high school literature class, Peter Bavis (as cited in Ogle, 2000) developed a form of Sketch to Stretch that works well for his students, 95%

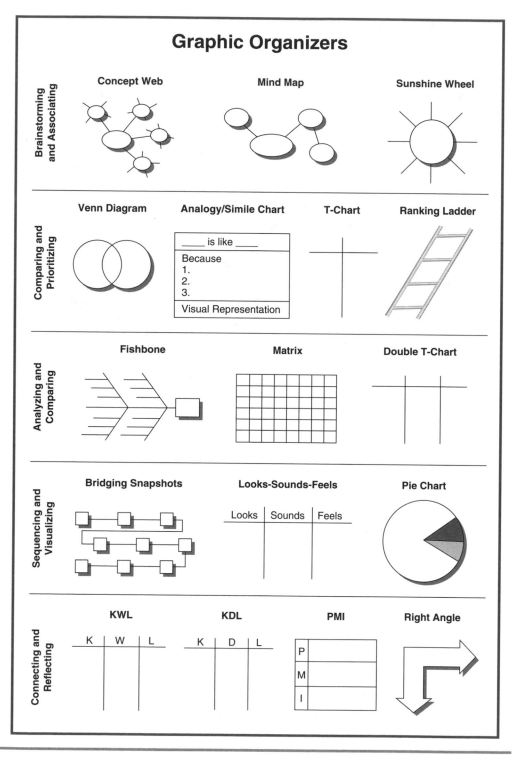

Figure 3.9

SOURCE: Adapted from *Brain-Compatible Learning for the Block* by R. Bruce Williams and Steven E. Dunn. © 2000 by Corwin Press. Reprinted with permission of Corwin Press, Thousand Oaks, CA.

of whom speak English as a second language. He has students work with partners in doing the activity. Each reads the poem or piece of literature individually and draws a sketch of what is important in the piece. When finished, partners share their drawings and discuss why they represented the text as they did. Their next step is to create a new, revised drawing that represents both of their ideas. These shared drawings then become their final version. Peter has found that his students return again and again to the texts as they try to create the best form of their interpretation.

Consolidating Ideas

Graphic organizers are tools that students can use to think about the text as a whole and how the main ideas relate to each other. Different graphic organizers serve different purposes (see Figure 3.9).

AUDITORY ENGAGEMENT

A very important way we make reading a priority in our classrooms is by reading aloud to students. This should be a part of a teacher's daily routine. When I ask teachers how many of them read aloud daily, I can almost predict that a high percentage of elementary teachers do this and enjoy it as a part of the shared life of the classroom. However, by middle school it occurs much less frequently. Probably the pace of the curriculum and the likelihood that there is a departmental structure, which limits time dramatically, are factors that make teachers less likely to find the time to read aloud. However, there are good times to read aloud even in a departmental structure. Take the following, for example:

• As students enter the classroom and start to settle down, read for three minutes from something in the news that relates to the topic or unit under study. Start with questions and then read about the topic from a "this week in the news" section or some magazine article.

• Jokes and humor are other great ways to get students' attention and start class on a positive note.

• Depending on the content, teachers find links to their teaching so students hear print language and vocabulary daily. This enhances their own potential for recognizing the same terms and concepts later in their studies and sets the model of reading being an important way to build knowledge and share humorous situations.

> ## Weekly Read-Aloud Checklist for Teachers
>
> This week I read orally from
> ☐ newspaper
> ☐ jokes and humorous stories
> ☐ magazines
> ☐ informational
> ☐ book/article
> ☐ fiction
> ☐ poetry
>
> **Figure 3.10**

If you have more time available, there are great extended readings that can build shared community knowledge. Students love to have an adult read special books aloud. One chapter a day or part of a chapter a day creates expectation and a focused time together. There are many good sources for such readings. One that is frequently used is Jim Trelease's *Read-Aloud Handbook* (2006). My one caution about this reference is that it includes mostly fiction. I think it is better to balance the reading of fiction with informational texts and humorous jokes, poems, and stories. If we want to model the range of reading that is available and accept the range of interests and tastes represented in any classroom, then including a broad range of readings is important. You can use a checklist like that shown in Figure 3.10 to be sure to vary your sources of read-alouds.

Remember to talk about what you read regularly and listen to students tell about their reading. In addition to school related topics, include items from

- community event fliers,
- organization newsletters,
- compact disc liner notes,
- shopping lists, and
- school bulletins.

Encourage students to bring items of interest, too. The more you are successful in your modeling of a variety of important literacy formats, the more students are likely to begin to share in these activities.

Student Oral Reading Forms

In addition to hearing a text read to them, many students find reading a text orally themselves an important element in their learning. We have already described one easy form of partner reading. Descriptions of several other good forms of oral reading follow.

Dynamic Duo Reading

This is a form of partner reading appropriate when there are clear character voices in a text. The two partners each assume a voice for their oral reading and select segments of the text to read that fit that perspective. For example, when students read a social studies text, they may take on the roles of TV anchorperson or newspaper columnist and participant in the events. When reading fiction, one student might assume the role of the narrator, and another the major character. Poetry works well for this kind of shared reading, especially poems for two voices.

Radio Reading

Students use the analogy of listening to the radio in this form of oral reading. The teacher divides the text to be read into sections and assigns a part to each student. The students are given time to prepare their oral reading, and if they need help they can turn to another student, the teacher, or a reference. They think about how to read the text so it sounds professional, like a radio commentator. After this rehearsal time the class proceeds to read. During the reading, only the reader has a book open. The other students listen, as if to a radio. One by one they take their turns, reading for the audience. The listeners are responsible for attending to and remembering what is said. They may make notes since they are accountable for knowing the content. When the reading is finished the teacher proceeds to help students reflect on the text, question, and respond.

Readers' Theater

Students love to be part of plays, yet they are very time consuming to produce and teachers know the pain of containing the energy and enthusiasm of students while preparing such events. The performance of readers' theater is easier. In this format the actors sit on chairs or stools and read their parts. They may use some piece of clothing to indicate their character, but they don't engage in full body movement. The scripts are rehearsed and then presented to the rest of the class or other audiences (other classes or retirement homes). Many good scripts are now available free on Web sites so teachers don't have to create their own versions from short stories, poetry, and novels.

Think-Alouds

Another powerful way teachers can grow students' oral strengths is by modeling the thinking that goes on when good readers engage with text. There is quite a bit written about "think-alouds" as a way to introduce active thinking (Davey, 1983; Wilhelm, 2001; Pressley and Afflerback, 1995). The teacher reads some segment of text orally and pauses periodically to express what is going on in his or her head. If the teacher also writes some key words on the board so students become familiar with the kinds of engagements that are most common, both the auditory and visual senses are stimulated and can support memory and use of the same activities by readers. Most teachers begin by expressing some connections they make with the text. Then they may also raise questions, express visual images that come to mind, and even comment on the author's craft.

As a way of getting started, the teacher may want to put the text on an overhead transparency to include more students. As some connection or question comes to mind, the teacher stops and writes on the margins of the transparency the comment or question so students can both hear and see the engagement. If there is text that suggests a strong visual image, the teacher can indicate what his or her mind's eye sees. Students could help identify the specific words and phrases that helped stimulate the visual image. With this kind of oral and visual support, students can learn to be more active in their own engagement with what they read. Later, they can be given sticky notes so they can also record their thinking and imaging on paper.

It may seem too obvious, but many students also love to get involved in books by hearing them read aloud on tape. Sometimes just hearing the first one or two chapters of a novel provides a needed jumping-off point for reluctant readers so they can get a sense of the meaning of a book without the strain of decoding the whole text. Once they have a good sense of the story they can read on independently. Some teachers have also found that just providing a musical background for students as they are reading independently helps them settle into the mood of a story more easily. If some students are distracted by outside noise, earphones can be used; even a student's own portable CD player can serve as a way to differentiate the auditory stimulation of the classroom.

ENGAGING PHYSICALLY

The physical component of learning (feeling something in your muscles) is rarely used by teachers. Engaging physically with text is easily done, however, by employing pantomime. Whirlwind, a program working with students in Chicago, uses children's natural interest in music and the arts to enhance students' connections with basic skills, including reading. Whirlwind's methods are strongly influenced by the idea that engaging physically with whatever one is trying to learn is a good idea. By interacting with text using dance and drama, students use their bodies to process the material. While this is physically engaging, it also engages the students visually by causing them to form pictures in their heads as they read. Nanci Bell's (2003) work as well as that of others has influenced the evolution of Whirlwind's programs. See Coming Together to Learn Through the Arts in Chapter 7 for a description of Whirlwind's methodology by its executive director.

MOTIVATING MIDDLE GRADE STUDENTS TO READ

One of the most frequently expressed concerns of middle grade teachers is that students seem to stop reading on their own. It is helpful in dealing with this problem to take a closer look at factors that affect motivation for adolescents. Among those that are significant are the following:

- interesting topics,
- degree of autonomy,
- peer interaction,
- self-efficacy,
- conceptual understanding, and
- successful experiences.

Interesting Topics

Young adolescents are in the beginning stages of discovering and investigating an expanding world; their curiosity and energy can be tapped best through materials that are connected to topics that already hold some interest to them. One middle school teacher has students study the twentieth century through self-selected, personal topics. Their reports have investigated the last century through topics such as the guitar, Lucille Ball, computers, dance, basketball, and so on. When students start with their own interests, the background of all else that happened takes on more significance to them.

Degree of Autonomy

Middle school students enjoy having a choice about what to read and write, as well as some control over the task. Part of this autonomy is developing one's own strengths as a learner and taking part in setting individual learning goals. This is a great time to have students develop a deeper understanding of what it means to read and to analyze their own strengths as readers. Doing surveys of their strategies, keeping logs of their reading, assessing their own vocabulary growth, and monitoring their fluency all fit with the needs of these students to know more about themselves and to make decisions about how to learn. It is especially appropriate at this age to have students create portfolios of their work so they can tangibly engage with the teachers in evaluating their learning.

Peer Interaction

Adolescents are very conscious of their peers and are very motivated by social interactions. Therefore, literacy activities that involve group work, cooperative teams, and ways to increase peer interaction are likely to motivate students more than regular individual assignments. At this stage, students look to their peers more than to adults, and teachers can support positive peer engagements by the activities we structure in the classroom. Book clubs, discussion groups, plays, and media productions developed by groups of students all can serve to support literacy.

Self-Efficacy

Belief in one's ability to succeed is a major component of motivation. Adolescents, as adults, are drawn to activities that make them feel good about themselves. Beliefs about our competence and control are the filters through which information is processed. As teachers we need to make sure that students can "save face" in all we ask of them. They need to know ahead of time what is going to be expected of them and have a clear sense of direction and evaluation. For young adolescents whose bodies don't seem under their control, having some predictability can do much to make them feel more comfortable. Involving them in evaluation of their own work is another way to increase a sense of self-efficacy.

Conceptual Understanding

Students at this age need to understand why they are doing the things we ask of them in school. They are able to enter into a more conceptual dialogue about learning and the purposes of literacy. We have found many students very interested in learning about the brain and how it functions. Making connections to literacy is easy. One high school reading teacher, Suzanne Zweig, has used an article by Cunningham and Stanovich (1998) to explain the importance of wide reading to her high school students. Many have found it fascinating to know more about the value of daily reading and the fact that vocabulary development depends on reading rather than oral forms of gaining information.

Teacher's Role in Ensuring Successful Experiences

Unlike younger children who often flock around their teachers and compete for time to tell about their interests and activities, adolescents are becoming more private, not as open to adults, and less interested in extended conversations with adults. Middle school and high school teachers need to sharpen their observational skills by watching and listening as students interact with one another and with instructional materials. What do they talk about and with whom? What makes them laugh? What are their moods? How do individuals respond to different class activities? What is their family makeup and cultural background? Adolescents often have unique struggles as they start to define themselves as individuals. We teachers can help all of our students grow in understanding by educating ourselves about various cultural communication styles, learning styles, and social norms for students in our community.

Given the diversity of our students and the changing nature of teen culture, literacy can play an important role in helping us all understand one another better. Books and articles about adolescents can be useful for teachers in understanding students, as well as for students in understanding each other. Many times these articles and books may be more personal than students want to discuss orally. In these cases some written responses may be useful. At other times shared reading may be enough.

WORKING WITH OTHER ADULTS IN THE CLASSROOM

Classrooms often have more than one adult in them as a result of the movement to meeting the needs of all learners within the regular classroom. Both students in Title I reading programs and students who are serviced under the Individuals with Disabilities Education Improvement Act (IDEA) spend as much of their time in the classroom as possible. This provides a real opportunity for classroom teachers, reading specialists, special education teachers, and aides to work together. However, for adults who are accustomed to working alone, the shift to teaming is not automatic. It takes a great deal of time and effort to make teaming effective for both the students and the teachers involved.

One of the immediate benefits is that there are more adult voices in the classroom. It permits teachers talking together about what they read and their interpretations of texts that are read in the class. Don't use your time as adults only to focus on the specific instructional goals for individual children, but take advantage of the modeling of literacy behaviors that two adults sharing classroom time makes possible. There are many children who have never heard adults talk about what they read, the kinds of materials they enjoy, or their questions about texts. If teachers can self-consciously find some stories or articles on which they disagree and share these responses with students, they will have created a great modeling opportunity. Students need to know that we don't read the same materials with the same interpretations or the same emotional responses.

Having more than one adult in the classroom also creates a wonderful opportunity for small group work and it especially makes some heterogeneous flexible groups easier to start. Children are often great working with others if teachers guide them in acting appropriately. Children can learn to support new readers and new English speakers if they receive help. Students can be great Reading Buddies for classmates with disabilities or as assistants in other classrooms. Some teachers have involved students in reading orally into tape recorders so students can quickly get the textbook or novel being used in the classroom. See Coming Together to Learn from Each Other for a firsthand account of students helping other students.

THE TEACHER AS READER

Most teachers and educators are readers. However, many of us forget to make that visible to children. If teachers make a special place where their reading material is kept, students can build an expectation that adults also read. I still recall my middle school teacher who had a small book rack on his desk. In it he kept the biography or other book he was reading (it changed very frequently), a dictionary he used almost daily, a thesaurus, a few magazines, and the daily newspaper nudged into a corner, always looking precariously balanced with the other substantial books. I think I learned to love *National Geographic* just because he often showed us pictures and maps and read snippets from pertinent articles. I have no doubt that Mr. Kidd was a reader; however, I don't have such vivid memories of other teachers as readers. If we make a point of it, we can be sure our students know when we buy a book as a gift for a friend, when we get a new magazine that discusses some timely occurrence like the Olympics or community celebrations, when we explore a Web site that provides current information, and when we find jokes and cartoons that are particularly enjoyable. Our students need to have reading brought to their attention regularly so they also begin to think as we do and make reading a regular part of their lives.

Coming Together to Learn From Each Other

Inclusion at Agassiz School

—Debbie Brown

The beginning of my teaching career meant one teacher alone in the classroom with her students. Although I became comfortable team teaching and had positive experience with inclusion, it took a long time before I agreed to a two-year program to include six students with autism in my fifth grade Chicago public school classroom. The scope of this project appeared to be too extensive for my ability. I imagined the worst: the responsibility would be too great, there would be 40 students in my class, there wouldn't be a second classroom to use, there would be no substitute if the special education teacher were absent. I thought only of the negatives. Luckily for me, my friend and colleague Janine Gray Hanna painted a different picture. She sold me on the benefits and the possibilities of such collaboration.

Once I agreed to try it out, the pieces fell into place. We would have two classrooms to use for our 32 students. This was crucial for the process to succeed. During part of each day we separated the students. Then each of us could teach lessons that weren't appropriate for inclusion. This separate classroom meant we could do reverse inclusion as well. Regular education students from my class loved to help out or just spend time there. Also, they could earn the privilege to go there for snack time. Not only would we have two classrooms to use, but also we would have the help from a talented and caring teacher assistant, Lucybeth Sierra. During the second year of our collaboration, money from a grant for Least Restrictive Environment paid for one hour a week of planning time done outside the school day. Although we would have done the planning regardless of this grant, it made us feel even more positive toward our work.

The beginning of the school year meant getting to know the strengths and abilities of all the students. I quickly adjusted my preconceived notions of autism. I learned that the condition has more parameters than I knew. For instance, the range of reading ability was from nonreader to graduate level of college. Don not only could decode at such an advanced level, but also he could tell the other students how to spell any word and could edit their papers. He even won the intermediate spelling bee with no special accommodations. Ricky had an incredible sense of humor and delighted us with his cartoons and songs. We were told Greg would never learn to read. After two years of this inclusion, he was able to decode at a fourth grade level. Sean was our expert on all sports, especially hockey. For every lesson in geography, he told us the name of the teams in that state. During our second year together, Daniel read constantly. He would read Harry Potter books aloud to anyone who would listen. Kenny's kindness and desire to help touched us all.

Many facets contributed to the success of this inclusion. Janine and I were both experienced teachers. We knew how to pace lessons and organize the class. We were committed to uncovering the strengths of all our students. We knew flexibility would be a key component, second to a sense of humor. Agreeing to be flexible meant there were times we had to quickly change our plans because one or more students had pressing needs. Most of our 20-minute lunches were spent together, although they were not always working lunches. Discussing other topics was often a refreshing break. It was also a time to reflect on what was working and what needed improvement. Although we had lesson plans for the week, we needed to meet every morning to fine-tune them.

Working with another teacher provided benefits that do not exist when one teaches alone. For example, while one of us taught the lesson, the other one could be coteaching, assisting, preparing the next lesson, attending a staffing, calling to arrange a field trip, or helping individual students. Having two teachers in the room reduced some of the stress of teaching. Spending so much time together led to a deepening of trust. We could point out areas that needed more focus without stepping on the other's toes.

There are many things that can be done to make the lessons work for students with special needs. Books on the same topic but written on an easier level were used whenever we did research projects. This was helpful for the regular education students as well because of their wide range of reading ability. Art was incorporated whenever possible. Students could create cartoons to share what they learned. Pictures with labels could be used. Each year included arts partnership units with professional artists and dancers. We worked very hard to develop hands-on lessons. Students learned math using carrots, watermelons, marshmallows, jelly beans, pancakes, Kool-Aid, and candy hearts, as well as more traditional manipulative. Science lessons were also centered on demonstrations and experiments. We created relief maps to learn about geography and searched for artifacts in our archaeological dig. After all hands-on activities, students would write a response and often read additional material. If a student with autism struggled with writing, another student would write down what the autistic student had to say. Longer-term projects worked well also. Every member of the small group could contribute something to the research and presentation. All the students enjoyed rehearsing and presenting plays and reciting poetry.

Flexible grouping was done throughout the day. When there was a student teacher in the room, we would have four adults to lead small groups for reading or math instruction. We could also make use of the second classroom to limit some of the distractions. Peer tutoring was used when appropriate.

Not everything runs smoothly in any classroom. We established a Friday class meeting time to work on problems and issues that occurred during the week. Sometimes we role-played to look for possible solutions. The meeting always included compliments and treats and time for the students to have some unstructured time together. There were times during the year that I would meet with the students with special needs alone, and Janine would meet with the regular education students. This was a time for the students to get educated about autism and learn how to work better with their peers. We let them know how proud we were of their help and caring. They in turn would acknowledge the strengths of the students with autism.

The past two years are ones I will never forget. We all experienced that different doesn't mean better or worse, just different. We all grew from this togetherness, celebrating success and shoring each other up when necessary. As I reflected at the end of the school year, I could say with confidence that I would do it again.

To Reflect

1. How do the ideas presented in Chapter 3 relate to your teaching experiences? What ideas support and confirm what you are already doing?

2. What did you find in this chapter that you can share with colleagues?

3. Did something suggest new possibilities for your program?

4. What questions does this chapter raise for further discussion and reflection?

Coming Next

Working Together With Students' Families

The Importance of Parental Influence

Working Productively With Parents
Understanding the Parent Community
A Rich Tapestry of Cultures and Values
Teacher Study Groups
Beyond Ethnic Differences
Taking Stock

Interpret the Curriculum for Parents
Parent Curriculum Night
Curriculum on a Page
Celebrate Learning: The Greek Festival
Special Reading Workshops for Parents

Keeping Parents Informed in Print Publications
A Primary Team's Communication With Parents

Coming Together to Build Bridges for Our Students' Parents and Their
Community: Literacy and the Community
Special Family Reading Projects
Parents as Reading Partners

Inviting Parents Into the School

Inviting Parents Into the Classroom

Parents as Reading and Writing Partners

Supporting Literacy Programs

Making Academic Connections
Family History

Our Families' Favorite Stories and Books

Connecting Through Home-School Journals and Portfolios
Student Work Portfolios
Student Weekly Summaries
Home-School Journals
Metacognitive Journals

Stimulating Ongoing Reflections With Home Links

Sharing the Life of the School

To Reflect

• • •

Working Together With Students' Families

4

THE IMPORTANCE OF PARENTAL INFLUENCE

Parents are their children's first teachers, and they continue to have an enormous influence over their children's learning throughout life. In telling the story of his childhood, Ben Carson, head of pediatric surgery at Johns Hopkins in Baltimore, illustrates the power of parental influence (Carson, 1996). Carson grew up without a father, and his mother had to work seven days a week to keep the children together. While cleaning homes of wealthier suburban families, she began to notice that they had lots of books and magazines in their homes. She contrasted that with her own home and realized that her children were not becoming readers. In fact, the boys were not interested and just watched a lot of TV. One day she came home and announced a new plan for the family: Each of the children would read for one-half hour each day. What an uproar, Ben recalls. However, as a result of her insistence, he began to read at home and became interested in the way books could transport him into new worlds. Eventually, he went on to college and became the first in his family to earn an advanced degree.

I like this personal story since it makes the point so clearly. When parents realize what is needed for their children, most want to respond. And when they do, their influence can be significant. Particularly in developing literacy, we know that the influence of the home is enormous, and the support parents provide begins early in children's lives. As children mature, parents' influence continues.

WORKING PRODUCTIVELY WITH PARENTS

Current research points very clearly to the role that parents play in the very first years of their children's lives in establishing the foundations for the development of literacy. Even by nine months children have distinguished which sounds are significant in the language spoken around them, and they have begun to ignore unimportant sound differences. As parents read to infants and toddlers, the children begin to understand that the language of books is different from spoken language, and they learn the structure of stories, even knowing the differences in stories and other kinds of written material. In a research study with young children (Ferreiro & Teberosky, 1982), children who had been read to could distinguish among the beginnings of stories, news articles, and informational pieces. Lap reading experiences are not only enjoyable ways to bond with young children, but they also help create strong positive emotional connections with reading for children. Children who begin their first years of schooling with rich and deep family reading experiences are most ready to begin reading themselves. They expect that they will become readers and know the variety of reasons reading is important in their family and community.

Once children are in school, parents continue to have an important role in the development of their literacy. Kindergarten through second grade children need regular experiences reading with their parents at home. The more they read, the better they get, so home reading reinforces what they are learning and builds their strength as readers. When parents reinforce the orientation to reading being used in the school, children are most helped in their goal of reading independently. For example, most primary teachers try to instill strategies that help students master active reading by having them first preview or do a picture walk to gain a sense of the whole. Then they teach children to check visual clues to confirm their interpretation of words and phrases and to learn a series of steps to unlock unfamiliar words. When parents read with their children and also reinforce these same strategic orientations, the children gain confidence through the consistent practices. Parents continue to be important in setting aside time for children to read independently and checking to see that they are enjoying the reading they do. Parents who see that there are books and magazines at home for children to read help support reading in yet another way. Those who buy books, subscribe to children's book clubs, and have children's magazine subscriptions that come regularly to the home create a rich literate environment for children. Because there are so many studies (National Assessment of Educational Progress [NAEP], Program for International Student Assessment [PISA], Reading Recovery) that demonstrate the critical role parents play in children's literacy development, it is important that schools work to strengthen the communication with parents and provide as much support as possible for this home-school partnership in developing children's literacy.

We as teachers and administrators need to think together about how we can work most productively with the parents in our particular schools. Each community is distinct, and what works in one area may not be the right approach in another. We need to be sensitive to particular norms and values of the families in our schools. The more we can partner with them, the more effective we will all be.

Understanding the Parent Community

If we are going to work together with parents and enlist their support in nurturing their children's reading, we need to know how to communicate

effectively with them. In some school communities this is easy, especially when teachers and families come from the same cultural backgrounds and have lived similar lives. More and more, however, students in our schools represent new, immigrant populations. Often the families come from unfamiliar cultures and bring with them experiences quite different from those of the teaching staff.

A Rich Tapestry of Cultures and Values

One of the exciting things about living is that we realize that most people are not just like us! It is amazing how different we all are. Where we share much in common, we also have developed a rich tapestry of individual and cultural variations. We as educators will become more effective as communicators if we take time to listen to our students' parents so we can involve parents effectively.

> ### Build Constructive Partnerships With Parents
>
> Think about what you (or your school) are doing to make parents feel welcome and involved. You may already have many initiatives under way, or individually there may be exciting things going on that others on the faculty might want to learn from. Make a list of what you are already doing. Then read the sections in this chapter and see if they stimulate further ideas and ways you can reach out. Make notes of your ideas in the margins so you do not forget them.

For example, in my own experience working with Hispanic families in Chicago, I have begun to appreciate some basic cultural differences that influence the relationships between parents and our schools. First, in getting to know a few Hispanic families, I learned how central the family is to their identity. These family members are very loyal and supportive of each other. If one member loses a job or needs help, the others come to that person's aid with little regard for the economic consequences to themselves. This sense of family and group identity translates into all aspects of life. When children enter school, parents want them to be good team players and not focus on their individual achievement as much. Individual competitions do not attract Hispanic children in our neighborhood, but team games do. In school we have found that even in reading groups, the children prefer to cooperate in genuine ways rather than have attention drawn to them. This is a well instilled cultural value.

Another deeply felt value that affects Hispanic children and teachers is the elevated status in which education is held. Mothers who are part of a Latino Outreach Project (Kelly, 2000) shared some of their tension with American educational assumptions after being in this country for three to five years. These mothers have great regard for teachers; they assume that teachers can do the best job of teaching their children English and reading. They did not understand why teachers wanted them involved in early literacy activities since the "school people" are trained for this. It took a great deal of sensitivity and many talks to persuade some of these mothers that they could and should support the literacy development of their children. Without taking time to understand the parents' value and respect for education, teachers had been critical of the passivity of parents when they were asked to help their children with homework tasks.

It is not easy to know when there are cultural differences. With children from many different cultures, religions, and personal histories, we can feel overwhelmed in trying to respect the variations. Yet, there are many resources to help us become more sensitive and build our own awareness of how our values are shaped by our particular histories. Begin by finding out as much as possible about the particular life experiences of our students. If there is a new immigrant population or a shift in housing patterns, we can spend some time focused on family and community identity and values (see Figure 4.1).

Much can evolve from our efforts to work together with parents. For example, one interesting ongoing project sponsored by WestEd, the Bridging Cultures Project (Quiroz, Greenfield, & Alchech, 1999) brings teachers and researchers together to apply research on cross-cultural value conflicts in schools to the education of the Latino students in their schools. One teacher analyzed their ways of conducting parent-student conferences and made several shifts over time in efforts to seek a culturally compatible

FOCUSING ON FAMILY AND COMMUNITY VALUES

- Invite a community member who can speak with the faculty and staff about the newcomers.

- Seek out the professional and religious resources in your own area. (For example, Illinois has the Illinois Resource Center, which is funded specifically to help educators deal with linguistic and cultural diversity in the state.)

- Get on the Internet and find information. Establishing some personal connections with educators in countries or regions from which your new student population has come can help you understand differences more easily.

- Read novels, children's books, and informational books about other cultures. Use videos and CD-ROMs to extend knowledge, too.

- Create a cross-cultural committee of parents and community members to meet regularly with the faculty and staff to explore ways to learn more and become more sensitive about one another.

- Connect with other projects that are exploring cultural sensitivity either directly or online.

- Make some home visits so you can talk to parents in their home environment. This can be a very important statement of your respect for them and your interest in their lives.

Figure 4.1

format for the conferences. Over time this teacher changed to having group conferences with several parents. She learned both that the Latino style is more group than individual and that students were uncomfortable with her model of having individual children lead the conference with the parents since they value adults as authority figures. After changing her conferences so children and parents came together in groups and then children led their parents to their own work portfolios, she concluded:

> The group conferencing was relaxing for the parents according to the teachers' report. It was a less threatening environment than the individual conferencing style; parents supplied support and were company for one another. This format provided a group voice from the parents rather than an individual voice. The conferencing time was also structured so that after one hour, parents could sign up for a private conference or ask a few questions without others present. (p. 69)

The Bridging Cultures Project illustrates one way teachers can continue to learn to be more effective in communicating with families by understanding their values and adjusting traditional school practices to them. The beginning point is taking time to reflect on the possible cultural mismatches that may exist between educators and parents. Rather than assume they do not exist, it is good to take stock periodically. Some faculties have surveyed parents using written forms to find out if there are ways to improve their communication. Some have contracted with consultants to do interviews with both faculty and parents to ascertain the same information. Some schools and districts have parent liaisons so differences in cultures do not block good working relations. Listening to students is another easy way to check the depth of communication that is effective between homes and school.

Teacher Study Groups

In setting staff development goals both personally and for a school team, attention to parents and community differences is an important area to highlight. Many creative and valuable projects have evolved as teachers have learned more about the cultures and values of their student families. A study group dedicated to discussing articles or books can make such learning a rich experience. You might start with *Supporting the Literacy Development of English Learners* (Young & Hadaway, 2006) or *Collaboration for Diverse Learners: Viewpoints and Practices* (Risko & Bromley, 2001) or *Teaching All the Children: Strategies for Developing Literacy in an Urban Setting* (Lapp et al., 2004).

Beyond Ethnic Differences

A reminder is also needed about three other areas of cultural difference affecting more of our families. The first is that many families are under great stress, with parents and caregivers working full time or more. Finding creative ways to communicate with them is also our responsibility and another aspect of cultural sensitivity. We cannot hold conferences always during the day and expect welcome responses from families who cannot be excused from work for school visits. Schools can do a lot to relieve the stress of parents by providing many different avenues for communication, for example, by moving conferences to a flexible schedule with some during the day, some in the evening, and some on weekends. Parents may find the Internet a good form of communication since it is available 24 hours per day. Other schools have used recorded telephone messages to facilitate communication on specific topics. Homework hot lines can help parents stay on top of what their children are doing.

Second, the school itself may not be a culturally welcoming place for parents who had bad experiences as students and have a great deal of negative emotions associated with entering school buildings. In one project, we met parents in the local church in the evening so we all were on more neutral turf and equally ill at ease at first. The parents were at home in the church and were in charge of providing some refreshments for the meeting. It gave them a sense of control that is missing when they enter a school building. In the church, the natural leaders of the parent community were expected to take a leading role and did so.

A similar caution about what happens when parents of different economic and social classes have children in the same school comes from a research study by Rogers and Tyson (2000). From interviews with parents, she learned that many working-class mothers were too intimidated to take part in the parent activities encouraged by the school. They felt the "tennis moms" were in control and did not feel invited to share their gifts. No changes would have been made in that school if time had not been spent listening to the parents to find out how they felt. This is such an important statement of respect. Once parents feel they are listened to, they can and will participate creatively in developing solutions.

The third concern is that women run most schools, and men may feel excluded. Boys' interests in reading are also different from most of their teachers'. The checklist provided in Figure 4.2 is worth using and then discussing with faculty. If this area is important, there are resources available to encourage more male participation in children's reading on the Internet and through organizations.

Taking Stock

Good parent-school relations are important. Yet differences in experiences and cultures mean that we should not assume one way of communicating will work for everyone, especially for families who have not had a long tradition of being part of our school culture or had success in school.

> ## Culturally Compatible Communication
>
> Educators need to
>
> - understand more about the culture of our students,
>
> - find ways to communicate comfortably with parents,
>
> - adjust our structures to meet the new family demands,
>
> - plan ongoing events and opportunities to involve families, and
>
> - find ways to show respect for the "funds of knowledge" and experiences of parents and bring them into the classroom.

IS YOUR SCHOOL FATHER FRIENDLY?

Here is a checklist to help you assess just how friendly your school is to fathers. If your school is not doing these things, or is not doing them well, now is a good time to start planning improvements. At your school, do you

_____ 1. Actively and continuously encourage all men to participate—regardless of their backgrounds, attitudes, limitations, or age?

_____ 2. Send a copy of notices to fathers not living in the home?

_____ 3. Tell men directly (not through mothers) that the school needs their involvement?

_____ 4. Display photos or drawings and publish stories of men involved with children at school?

_____ 5. Show a genuine interest in fathers by greeting them at the door and asking them casual questions, like, "So what have you been up to lately?"

_____ 6. Give both dads and moms specific activities to do with their children at home, and ask them to do specific "jobs" at school?

_____ 7. Find out what men are interested in, what they would like to do, and what information, help, or skills they need?

_____ 8. Provide programs and activities geared to meet the specific needs of fathers and other significant male adults in students' lives?

_____ 9. Schedule home visits, conferences, and other events at a time when fathers can attend?

_____ 10. Call or visit men when they don't attend a planned event and ask them why?

_____ 11. Speak to mothers and fathers equally when they are both present at meetings, conferences, or home visits?

_____ 12. Offer something that is unique for men only, like a "Fathers' Club" or weekly "Donuts for Dads" coffees?

_____ 13. Include in the parent room *Sports Illustrated*, special books and notices for dads, and other items of interest to men?

_____ 14. Use men to recruit fathers and other male volunteers in the community?

_____ 15. Recognize dads' contributions, as well as moms'?

Figure 4.2

SOURCE: Adapted from *Keys to Success for Urban School Principals* by Gwendolyn J. Cooke. © 2002 by Corwin Press. Reprinted with permission of Corwin Press, Thousand Oaks, CA.

Specifically to support literacy, we also need to help parents understand what they can do and how important their role is in reading and writing development. We can also help them learn to read effectively with their children, find books appropriate for them, and engage in "book talk" or oral sharing of stories and family events that can lead into inquiry projects and writing.

INTERPRET THE CURRICULUM FOR PARENTS

Because there are so many ways parents can support their children in becoming good readers during their school years, we need to ensure that we do all we can to develop strong programs and expand current efforts that connect parents with their children. All parents are interested in their children doing well in school. Yet many do not know how to evaluate their successes or development. Many do not understand what teachers do to teach reading. There are many ways schools can help parents understand the way the school and particular grade level classrooms function. This is particularly important when schools have immigrant families who are unfamiliar with American schools. However, it is also important for all families, particularly since curriculum and school expectations keep changing. Parents need to understand the reasons for new approaches to literacy, the role of standards and outcomes, and the focus on assessment.

Parent Curriculum Night

A good way to explain the curriculum to parents is to have special parent nights where new focuses of the curriculum are introduced and explained and even where parents have opportunities to try out the innovations as learners themselves. Northbrook (Illinois) School District 27 has parent curriculum nights for each area of the curriculum. At these events teachers model their instructional approaches, and families participate in a range of typical classroom activities under the teachers' leadership. The district has found much better support from families who have an understanding of the instructional program. Parents engage in literature discussions and inquiry activities and even may construct a shared story while they are seated in their child's classroom with the teacher leading the class. Rather than hearing about the ways reading is taught, the parents experience it firsthand. For most parents the current literacy instructional groupings and ways of using literature to develop reading and writing are unfamiliar, and they can gain a much better understanding of what teachers are doing and why by participating actively in these events. See Figure 4.3 for an example of how teachers at the Northbrook school district organize this family reading day event.

In some middle and secondary schools, parents follow their child's schedule for the day and have brief 10–15 minute classes with each instructor explaining his or her program as part of the orientation to the school. This gives parents a clear idea of what the academic program is like and the rapidity with which students have to move from one area to another, both physically and mentally. This activity is useful for parents from abroad, since in many countries students do not change rooms—instead, the teachers do. In Spain, for example, a group of 20–30 students stays together in the same classroom for the full year, and teachers rotate in and out. The array of subjects rotates too, with only some subjects taught each day; students will have a different schedule on Monday than on Tuesday. These differences make it important that parents as well as students have a good understanding of how our schools function.

Curriculum on a Page

Accountability and adherence to state and local standards have taken on much more importance in the last few years. Some districts have used the standards focus as a way of involving parents in the development of aligned curriculum and instruction. Parents serve on the committees and are resources to parent groups in the community to interpret the changes. One way to help parents understand the curriculum is to create grade level documents with the curriculum goals highlighted on a single page (see Figure 4.4).

Celebrate Learning: The Greek Festival

Parents also understand what and how their children are learning when they participate by celebrating students' accomplishments. Schools often show off the culmination of units of study and special projects with special events. Parents from all cultural groups like to see their children's successes. They will more likely come to events where their children are "performing" than to sober conferences dealing with what is not happening. We have included an example from a sixth grade team's integrated language arts and history unit. As a culminating celebration of the team's study of ancient Greece, families are invited to an evening to view the projects and watch a program put on by the students as they share what they have learned. See Figure 4.5 showing a letter that is sent home to explain this special event about ancient Greece.

Family Reading Day

Session 1: 2:00 – 2:35 pm
Session 2: 2:40 – 3:15 pm
Session 3: 3:20 – 3:55 pm

Grade	Teachers	Room	Literature	Strategies
K	Jack Smith Judy Burr	108	*Goggles* by Ezra Jack Keats	Language Experience Approach: Beginners learn to use their own knowledge, experience, and language to help construct meaning from the printed word. Sketch-to-Stretch: Students generate sketches or pictures that relate to a story and then share and discuss them with a group.
1	Kim Jera Ray Finn	106	*Swimmy* by Leo Lionni	Story Map: Students identify and visually organize the structure and content of a story. Directed Reading Thinking Activity: Students actively participate in the reading process by making and revising predictions during reading.
2	Debbie Durg Liz Yeder	103	*Ira Sleeps Over* by Bernard Waber	Webbing: Students graphically organize information they have learned/heard from what was read. Written Conversation: Students and teachers explore meaning with one another through informal written communication.
3	John Brine Barb Liska	117	*Sarah, Plain and Tall* by Patricia MacLachlan	Reader's Theater: Students create a script from a narrative text and perform it for an audience. Say Something: Students respond to what has been read. Students express what they learned from the passage or text and tell how it relates to their own experiences.

Figure 4.3

CURRICULUM ON A PAGE

READING and LITERATURE

- Recognizes and uses vocabulary related to specific content areas.
- Recognizes that many words have multiple meanings.
- Uses structural analysis and context clues to determine word meanings.
- Uses the dictionary to locate words and to determine word meanings.
- Understands the main idea of a reading selection.
- Sequences events of a selection.
- Uses specific details to support and construct meaning.
- Identifies speakers in a dialogue.
- Predicts possible outcomes in a reading selection.
- Compares and contrasts information in text.
- Considers solutions to problems in a reading selection.
- Recognizes various traits of characters in literature.
- Distinguishes fiction from nonfiction.
- Identifies cause and effect relationships in a selection.
- Reads and analyzes various literary genres.
- Recognizes story elements such as: plot, setting, characterization, and theme.
- Recognizes figurative language in literature.
- Understands themes in literature.

MATHEMATICS

- Connections.
- Maintains recall of basic math facts.
- Uses estimation as a problem-solving procedure.
- Applies different types of problem-solving strate ies.
- Simplifies algebraic expressions.
- Completes function tables and finds function rules.
- Recognizes and uses metric units of measure.
- Performs addition, subtraction, multiplication, and division of integers.
- Identifies, analyzes, and solves problems using algebraic equations.
- Interprets a set of data using mean, median, mode, and range.
- Interprets and constructs different types of graphs.
- Identifies and classifies triangles, special quadrilaterals, and angles.
- Finds greatest common factors and least common multiples.
- Maintains addition, subtraction, multiplication, and division of fractions.

WRITING/GRAMMAR

- Uses meaningful prewriting strategies (thinking, mapping, notetaking, webs, reading, dialogue).
- Organizes ideas into paragraphs for essays, reports, and other writing activities.
- Develops writing to include sufficient and meaningful details, support, and elaboration.
- Develops meaningful introductions and conclusions.
- Uses the thesaurus for discovering new words.
- Supports text comprehension with facts and details.
- Revises, dialogues, and edits with peers.
- Reads, rereads, reflects, and reconsiders own text for revision and self-editing.
- Uses figurative and vivid language, including personification, alliteration, imagery, symbolism, similes and metaphors, hyperboles, and irony.
- Continues to use the library to develop library skills for research and report information.
- Uses various genres for expression.
- Recognizes and uses parts of speech correctly.
- Eliminates fragments and run-on sentences in writing.
- Uses and punctuates dialogue correctly.
- Uses colons, semicolons, and hyphens correctly.
- Uses direct objects, indirect objects, sentence beginnings, comparatives, and superlatives correctly.
- Uses indefinite pronoun and verb agreement.
- Uses irregular verbs.
- Demonstrates appropriate speaking behavior: articulate rate, volume, and body language.
- Recognizes purposes of oral messages (convey information, entertain, give directions, persuade).
- Makes inferences and identifies different points of view in oral messages.
- Participates in both large and small group discussions.
- Communicates ideas and feelings appropriately in formal and informal situations.
- Recalls specific and significant details of an oral passage.
- Enjoys listening to and sharing writing with a variety of audiences.

SPELLING

- Spells the seventh grade high-frequency word list correctly.
- Knows and uses all seventh grade rules and spelling generalizations.
- Applies spelling rules in writing.
- Uses a variety of resources to verify standard spelling (e.g., the dictionary).

Figure 4.4

THE SIXTH GRADE'S ANNUAL GREEK FESTIVAL

THURSDAY, FEBRUARY 24TH

6:00–9:00

- Be astounded by student displays created as part of our interdisciplinary unit on ancient Greece.

- Watch the drama and game portion of the evening in the gym starting at 6:45.

- Enjoy specially prepared Greek treats.

- Remember that every sixth grader should be in Greek costume.

If you cannot attend and cannot provide a ride to the event for your child, please let the sixth grade team know and we will arrange a ride for him or her.

See you there!

Figure 4.5

Special Reading Workshops for Parents

While a single evening in school can be useful in helping parents understand the instructional program or see the results of units of study, providing a series of workshops can really deepen parents' understanding and sharing in reading with their children. We include an example of a four-week workshop series done by reading specialist Joyce Doolin for parents of primary children. The setting was made very appealing with a light supper. Children and parents came together so the ways children were learning were made very clear to parents. The possibility of better talk between parents and children about reading was one of Joyce's goals, so she wanted to stimulate that during the workshops. As a result of this extended workshop series, Joyce got to know the parents better and was able to build some more personal relationships with them.

KEEPING PARENTS INFORMED IN PRINT PUBLICATIONS

Parents in most communities are very interested in the kinds of instruction being provided. Even with open houses and curriculum nights, the implemented curriculum in the classroom keeps developing over the course of the year. This is especially true in the first and second grade literacy curriculum since the literacy abilities of children in those grades increase so rapidly.

A Primary Team's Communication With Parents

To keep parents of young children informed about the reading and writing program in their shared multiage classroom is an important goal of teachers Debbie Gurvitz and Debbie Shefren at Lyons School in Glenview, Illinois. They use multiple ways to maintain ongoing communication with parents. They send newsletters home twice a month, send regular Home Links to build connections between specific instruction and homework, have volunteer parents working in their classroom regularly, and use parent-child-teacher conferences twice a year. Parents and children help set goals together at the fall conference and engage in reflection in the spring. At the open house nights, parents can see examples of the children's work since each child shares his or her portfolio of work. These serve to inform parents about each child's progress and the kinds of work experiences they have had. Each of these opportunities builds a closer connection between school and home and answers concerned parents' questions.

The bimonthly newsletter is the most frequent communication. One side provides general information about classroom events. The second side is used to provide a more in-depth explanation of research in literacy that provides the foundation on which their program is based. The two Debbies added this second side two years ago to inform parents and reassure them that the classroom is in compliance with best practices in teaching. They cite new research and explain how classroom practices reflect this knowledge. They also suggest ways parents can support their instruction at home.

Another important tool for communication and involvement of parents is the teachers' Home Links. These are sent when the teachers have specific roles they want parents to play in helping their children learn particular strategies or content. For example, in the fall they send a Home Link regarding how to read with a young child. As they develop an orientation to word study with the children, the teachers also want the parents to reinforce their orientation to words. Therefore, they send a Home Link with very specific ideas about how parents can support the curriculum. An example of a Home Link is shown in Figure 4.6.

HOME LINK: WORD STUDY

As part of our word study program, children sort words by word families. Today we completed our second word sort activity. The *ap* and *ab* word families were introduced.

To reinforce the words introduced, please complete this activity at home. After sorting and reading the words, rubber band together and place in a box for future use.

Throughout the year your child will be adding to his or her word sort collection. This is an excellent reading and phonics reinforcement of consonant and vowel sounds, word patterns, and rhyming words.

To complete a word sort,

1. Have the children cut out each card.

2. Mix up the cards.

3. Place the cards face down.

4. Pick a card.

5. Say the word.

6. Put it in a column (*at* or *am*).

7. Pick the next card. Place it in the appropriate column.

8. Each time you add a word to the column, read the entire list of words.

9. After sorting these cards, mix in the *am* and *at* words. Sort by *ab, ap, am,* and *at.*

10. After sorting the cards, play again or put away for safe keeping.

11. KEEP AT HOME.

Figure 4.6

READING WORKSHOPS TO BEGIN

Beginning Wednesday, October 18th, Oakton's reading specialist and our intensive reading teacher will begin a series of four workshops for Oakton parents and their children. Each parent must be accompanied by at least one of their children. Together, they will learn some strategies for working together. At the beginning of each session (6:30 – 7:00 pm) a light meal will be provided. Classes will begin at 7:00 pm and end at 8:30 pm. The following topics will be presented:

Oct. 18 – Beginning Reading/Learning and Using New Words

Oct. 25 – Learning to Understand What We Read

Nov. 1 – Keeping the Facts in the Right Order

Nov. 8 – Use Your Imagination

We promise that you will have fun together and learn something new about how YOUR child learns.

You will have to sign up ahead of time so that we will know how many people to prepare food and work materials for. A special certificate of achievement will be given to parents and students who attend all four workshops. Please return your sign-up sheet to us as soon as possible.

PARENT-STUDENT WORKSHOP

My child and I will participate in the parent-student workshop.

_____

Parent's Name

_____

Participating Student's Name

_____

Student's Homeroom Number

Return this form to school as soon as possible.

Figure 4.7

FAMILIES READING TOGETHER

Dear Oakton Parents,

At our recent Open House, Oakton School described a parent involvement program called FAMILIES READING TOGETHER. This is one of our programs to help demonstrate that learning must be a partnership between home and school.

In order to be part of this exciting program, you only need sign and return the pledge in which you agree to have 30 minutes of uninterrupted reading with your children each day. When we receive your signed pledge, we will send you the following items:

1. hints for success,

2. a reading record sheet for writing down what you read each day, and

3. a form to nominate your favorite books for others to read.

Whenever you fill up a reading record sheet, return it to school with your child and get a fresh one. More than 100 families have already joined us. After the regular parent conferences in November, prizes will be given to all families who participate, and those who read the most books will receive something very special. Join Oakton: FAMILIES READING TOGETHER now.

Good Reading!
Intensive Reading Specialist

OAKTON: FAMILIES READING TOGETHER

I, _____, hereby pledge to spend 30 minutes per day in uninterrupted family reading in my home.

Names of Students at Oakton   Homeroom

_____   _____

_____   _____

_____   _____

_____   _____

Parent Signature _____

Return this form to school as soon as possible.

Figure 4.8

READ WITH YOUR CHILD: A GUIDE FOR PARENTS

Fiction and short stories:

- Preview the book together and discuss pictures and any titles.

- Share the oral reading of the text—you read a page and then your child reads one.

- Encourage your child to make predictions about what will happen and how characters will react to new situations, and share your own ideas about the direction the story is taking.

- Discuss connections you make between the book and your own experiences or other books and movies you and your child share.

Nonfiction, magazines, and newspaper articles:

The weekend paper is a great source of articles that you and your children can share. Rather than newspaper reading being a solitary experience, get comfortable and take some time with your child to look through the sections of the paper that might be of interest to you both. As you scan the sections, find some high-interest articles. Either read the article orally to your child or share the reading of the text. Then discuss what you liked and learned from it. Encourage your child to find an article he or she finds interesting and read that together, too. You may be surprised at how many different articles you will both find interesting.

Figure 4.9

Coming Together To Build Bridges for Our Students' Parents and Their Community

Literacy and the Community

—Pat McCarthy

East Prairie School District 73 is a one-school district in Skokie, Illinois—a suburb just north of Chicago. It is part of Niles Township, which includes elementary schools in a number of cities and towns, two high schools, and a community college that serves a wider community than the township. Over the past 15 years, the area has become increasingly diverse, with more than 30 different languages spoken by area residents. This has presented cultural and educational challenges to the community. East Prairie has helped address these challenges by providing English language classes for parents and other adults living in the area.

East Prairie School District's adult education program began in 1988 through collaboration of its superintendent, Ron Bearwald, and Oakton Community College's Marilyn Antonik. There have been several different superintendents since that time, but Antonik continues to coordinate the greater community's adult literacy programs with warmth, humor, and compassion. In some ways, the partnership between Oakton and East Prairie is typical of such programs. Oakton supplies trained volunteer tutors, and the local coordinator sends back paperwork such as testing results, progress, and attendance in compliance with Oakton's grant requirements. What has made East Prairie's program different from others is that many tutors were homegrown; that is, the volunteers were parents, teachers, and residents of East Prairie or with direct ties to this community. In the early years of the program, adult students were not fully integrated into the East Prairie School community, even after they had received GEDs, mastered skills, or moved into better jobs.

More recently, a change has become obvious: Parents from various backgrounds and cultures are now a constant presence in the school as classroom volunteers, chaperones for field trips, committee members, and leaders. What is really important is that a number of students and former students in the adult education program who are presently learning or have learned to communicate in English are becoming an increasingly active part of the East Prairie School community. Noticing this enhanced participation of parents and relatives in school activities motivated me to reflect on some changes that have occurred over the years.

In my experience, this connection between literacy and community is not at all unusual. Not only do English classes for adults serve the obvious purpose of helping them master the language, but also they quite often serve as a vehicle for their integration into the school and larger community. That is not surprising, however, as communication is the key to participation and cooperation.

Special Family Reading Projects

Parents can be important partners in motivating children to read regularly. Some teachers create special events to focus parents and children on the value of reading regularly at home. These can be individual classroom projects or involve the whole school. See Figure 4.7 for an example of an all-school family reading project. Figure 4.8 shows how another school created a focus on families reading together. Parents are introduced to the importance of encouraging daily reading and are given a record keeping form that they sign off on each time the child reads. The forms usually are for one week, with signatures needed each day indicating that the child has read and the number of minutes he or she was engaged.

Parents as Reading Partners

There are advantages to having parents read along with all levels of children. Giving parents of young children specific ideas about how to encourage sharing around book reading is useful. As children become more independent in their own reading, a guide can help parents (see Figure 4.9).

INVITING PARENTS INTO THE SCHOOL

Some schools realize that many parents feel uncomfortable in schools. Building bridges for these parents can help create a more supportive relationship for the full course of children's schooling. Several good examples of how this can work exist. See Coming Together to Build Bridges for Our Students' Parents and Their Community for an example. Described by Pat McCarthy, it was developed as a response to a major shift in the population in her school district.

INVITING PARENTS INTO THE CLASSROOM

Once parents have an understanding of the curriculum, then some real involvement in class activities can support teachers' efforts. Finding a role for parents in classrooms takes some careful thinking and planning. If you are lucky enough to work in an area where there are parents who can come into the school, then it is worth the effort to think of how they can be most effective and at the same time have a pleasant experience themselves. For example, one does not build great relations if an eager parent is

READING GUIDELINES FOR PARENTS

Use the following suggestions to make reading an enjoyable and rewarding experience for you and your "buddy."

- Play little word games with your child. Make up a sentence and leave out a word; for example, *I went to the doctor because I was _____*. Ask your child to tell you what the missing word should be and why.

- Before reading a book aloud, ask your child questions about the story that can be answered by looking at the pictures.

- Read poems and nursery rhymes and leave out a rhyming word. Have your child guess the missing word and explain how he or she got the answer.

- Have your child look only at the pictures of a well-illustrated book and then ask him or her to make up a story to go with them.

- As you read aloud, leave out a word from a sentence (nouns work best) and ask your child to "fill in the blank." Ask your child to identify which clues in the sentence helped him or her identify the missing word.

- As you read aloud, make a silly mistake that affects the meaning of the sentence. See if your child notices and corrects you. If not, stop reading and think aloud as you correct your mistake. This will help your child to self-monitor while reading.

- While reading together, have your child look at a paragraph in the story and find all the words that have a specific letter combination; for example, all words ending with *-ing*.

Happy Reading!

Figure 4.10

only asked to use the copy machine hour after hour. There are some parents who are very eager to do whatever possible and need clear directions about how they can be helpful. Some parents have never worked with children in groups and need direction on how to maintain the discipline and group processes that the teachers have carefully worked to achieve. At times parent volunteers have created communication problems through critical comments and stories caused by their misperceptions of what the teacher was trying to achieve. When negatives get spread, they can be unnecessarily damaging to those involved. Therefore, involving parents in classroom activities deserves the concerted effort of the professional staff. What one teacher does, others need to think through so there aren't significantly different opportunities from one classroom or grade level to another.

PARENTS AS READING AND WRITING PARTNERS

Parents can be great support for the literacy program in a variety of ways. In the primary grades there is always a need for older readers to listen and read along with young children as they make sense of print. (Parents, community volunteers, and older children from upper grades all play important roles in being reading partners.) Teachers should provide specific instructions for how these reading buddy sessions are handled. Most teachers want the children to do the work of making meaning from text and need to instruct the volunteers not to interfere and provide too much support (see Figure 4.10). Jeannine Crockett, a first grade teacher at Ranch View Elementary in Naperville, Illinois, has effectively used parent volunteers to listen to children read orally. She has developed a simple form that the parent volunteers fill out as they work with each child. The parents give feedback on what the child has read, how fluently each book was handled, and the way the child dealt with errors or miscues. Finally, at the bottom of the form there is space for observations and questions (see Figure 4.11).

With the increasingly large range of reading abilities in classrooms, there is also an important role for volunteer parents to help provide the added time some students will need to master what others can learn quickly. They can work with them individually or in small groups in the classroom and relieve the teacher for other responsibilities. The key is that parents support and reinforce what the children have already learned. They are not there as teachers but as aides when the children need to practice. Parents have the power to make their children fans of reading or they can make reading seem like a chore.

PARENT VOLUNTEER FORM

Literacy Volunteer: _____

Student Name: _____

Date: _____

Record all books that are read to you aloud.

Level	Book title	Smooth	Word by word	Labored	Number of words missed and not self-corrected	Engagement with text

Observations and Questions:

Figure 4.11

SOURCE: Used with permission from Jeanine Crockett.

Parents can also be very helpful by supporting children's composing and writing. At the first level they can learn to take dictation from children. Again, the ground rules need to be clear for both student and adult. The two should sit side by side so the child can watch the writing and learn from the modeling. The adult needs to honor the child's own word and sentence choice. The adult should not edit and correct either grammar or ideas the child wants to express. In many classrooms parents are also a great help with the computers as children begin to express their own ideas using computer programs. Many times I have seen parents straighten out problems with computers and save teachers a great deal of energy.

SUPPORTING LITERACY PROGRAMS

In addition to helping directly as children learn to read and write, parents can also keep the resources for literacy in order. They can do much to help maintain classroom libraries and restock books and materials as children finish using them. Collecting new materials for upcoming units of study and creating hands-on activities are also places where teachers can use help and parents can be effective. Sometimes parents create a network and find out from one another who possesses some special items or personal artifacts that can enhance the class study.

MAKING ACADEMIC CONNECTIONS

Parents can support the academic content, too. When teachers inform parents of upcoming themes or special topics of study, the parents can be encouraged to visit and share what they have or serve as experts for the class. For example, when one class was studying the life cycle, a parent who works with butterflies came to class and explained his work. He brought some live chrysalises with him and a book showing some of the varieties of butterflies he knows. The children were fascinated.

Kaser and Short (1997) describe how they elicited from children topics of interest to them and then built inquiry units around those familiar interests. They were able to tap into the expertise of the parents in their Hispanic community and brought some of these parent experts in to help the class learn. The results went well beyond the specific project; the parents felt validated as valuable contributors to the school and recognized for what they knew.

At the upper elementary level, one teacher realized that her students thought of World War II as something totally unconnected to their lives.

Therefore, she surveyed the students' parents and found a grandfather who was willing to come in and share his experiences as a soldier during that war. For some of the children, it was the first time they had thought about what they were studying in history as having a link to their lives. The grandfather loved being the expert for the class and spent a good amount of time finding artifacts and pictures that would help the children make a real connection to the stories he told.

Family History

Some schools have had wonderful experiences studying the family histories of the students in the classroom or whole school. Parents and children together create a family autobiography. They collect pictures that show their family in different generations, going as far back as possible. They write stories of the lives of family members that sometimes come from interviewing older members. In some cases there are long-distance phone calls to clarify aspects of the family history and the family tree. Each student produces his or her own family autobiography and illustrates it with drawings and photographs. These are then displayed either in the library, in the halls of the school, or in the classrooms so all visitors may read and see the histories the children have to share. Again, there must be some thought given to this idea before starting out. If there are children who are not able to access their own histories the project may not be possible. These students can research the family trees of a famous person, such as an author or musician, instead.

Most schools will find this kind of literary activity stimulating and productive and that it helps to create a sense of community and familiarity among the students and teachers. *History Comes Home: Family Stories Across the Curriculum* (1999) by Zemelman, Bearden, Simmons, and Leki is a valuable resource for those looking for ways to use family histories in their classrooms.

OUR FAMILIES' FAVORITE STORIES AND BOOKS

Another way to involve families in classroom life is to ask parents to come to class and share either a favorite story that is told in the family or to read a favorite family book to the children.

Debbie Gurvitz asks parents to select a favorite poem with their child and write it on a Home Link. Then the child shares that poem with the whole class, and the Home Links are put on the bulletin board. At other times parents come in and read these favorites to the students.

At the upper levels, it can be interesting for parents to share the literacy histories of their families with students so the importance of literacy becomes more real. Many parents are delighted with the opportunity to bring in favorite and cherished books—sometimes collections of poetry that have been in the family for generations. My father brought some cherished beginning readers that he had used as a child to the class. How surprised the class of fifth graders were when they saw that the books were in Swedish and not English, even though he had attended school in the United States.

These activities are given to help stimulate your thinking of ways you too can involve families in thinking more consciously about the role of literacy in their lives. When you create such events, literacy as a lifetime activity becomes more visible and can be celebrated in the school. For some children it may be the first time they have really thought about literacy as an essential part of their lives. What a good beginning for a lifetime of reflection on and attention to reading. Teachers can follow personal reflections with autobiographical sketches of famous people who tell about their own reading lives to make a rich connection of reading for students.

CONNECTING THROUGH HOME-SCHOOL JOURNALS AND PORTFOLIOS

Many parents are just too busy with their work to have time to join the classroom activities during the day. We have already shared one way parents can help their children outside of normal classroom hours: by identifying favorite poems and writing them for their children. There are many similar activities you can use to create a dialogue between parents and school. Think of ways you have already used to build these bridges. While she was teaching first grade, Jane Hunt became frustrated that the children seemed to forget the great adventures they had had in school by the time they arrived home and their mothers asked, "What did you do in school today?" She decided to spend the last few minutes of the class day with the children on the rug while she composed a daily journal on a big notepad. By reviewing with the students what they had done during the day the students' were able to recall and then later retell for their parents much more about their school activities. Later in the year the children began to keep their own journals, writing in them just before the end of the school day. This practice helped to enormously increase the communication between children and parents. At the parent conferences in the spring, Jane too was delighted that parents seemed very aware of all the children were doing and very happy with the conversations they could have within the family.

STUDENT WEEKLY SUMMARIES

Week _____   Your name: _____

                      Parent: _____

Write about something you read.	Parent Response (ideas/questions)
Were you organized this week? Write about it.	Parent Response (ideas/questions)
Write about how you are doing in the area of listening. What will you work on?	Parent Response (ideas/questions)
Write about how you feel about math and why.	Parent Response (ideas/questions)

Figure 4.12

Student Work Portfolios

A valuable way to enhance communication is to send home student work each week. Many schools now have student folders or portfolios that move from school to home and back again each week. The teacher may write a note each week summarizing what the class has done and giving parents an idea of what will be upcoming.

Student Weekly Summaries

While parents appreciate knowing from the teacher what is happening in the classroom, it is also useful to have their children share their own evaluations of what they are learning and how they are performing as students. Some teachers in Glenview, Illinois, have involved the children in evaluating their accomplishments of the week on a simple interactive form (see Figure 4.12). The teacher prepares a weekly summary form, and students write their own reflections. Parents respond with their comments and then return the sheet with the portfolio on the following Monday.

Home-School Journals

At the middle level, teachers can simply have a journal that goes between school and home in which the students write personal reflections on what was significant during the week and how they felt about learning. Some teachers use a format that has the children then ask their parents a question coming out of the work that is being done. (For example, when the fifth graders were studying rock formations, one asked in her journal, "Mom, have you ever collected any rocks? Do you know how to identify igneous rocks?")

Parents are to read the journal and respond to the weekly entries. This helps build a closer connection between the home and the school and does so in a fairly easy way for the teachers, students, and parents.

Metacognitive Journals

As students get older, in middle school and high school, communication with parents is more difficult to stimulate. However, if there is an accepted practice of using journals and portfolios in place as part of the regular school routine, it can be sustained at the upper levels too. Often conferences with parents involve sharing student portfolios and reflections on their work. The Mundelein High School English department, for example, has students keep metacognitive journals of their learning and strategy use. These are tangible records that stay with the students and are used for personal reflection and evaluation throughout high school (Szymkoiak, 1998).

STIMULATING ONGOING REFLECTION WITH HOME LINKS

Another way teachers are creating closer ties to parents as students study and learn is to provide specific connections during units of instruction. Gurvitz (1999) involves her kindergarten parents regularly in literacy. Each month she focuses on a genre or an author study. At the beginning of each, she sends a Home Link asking parents to talk with their children and identify a favorite piece of literature or poem related to the theme. Each month she also has a content unit (building informational literacy) and asks parents to discuss particular questions with their children and help them do research and come back to class as an "expert" on the child's chosen question. Gurvitz learned that parents needed very explicit directions on how to work with their young children in this kind of research. Therefore, she devised a very structured approach to the Home Link. By being this explicit, the research shifted from parents doing most of the work to the children having the fun of learning how to learn.

The first and second grade team of Debbie Shefren and Jan Kirch also involves parents in helping the children learn. During their units they also send home Home Links that include a variety of kinds of learning activities for parents and children to do together. For example, during the study of plants, one link asked the family to identify things found in a garden, either theirs or a neighbor's (see Figure 4.13). Another week the task was to survey someone in the neighborhood about gardening (see Figure 4.14). With these kinds of activities, the families became a real part of the school curriculum.

SHARING THE LIFE OF THE SCHOOL

These specific examples from teachers should stimulate your own thinking about ways you can link parents and families more directly in your curriculum. The results are worth it. Children need to see what they do in school related to their homes. They need to get in the habit of sharing what they are learning, as a way of deepening that learning and as a way of bringing it closer to their own lives. The modeling that comes from parents and teachers and children sharing the life of school and celebrating specific accomplishments can last a lifetime!

GARDEN OBSERVATION CHECKLIST

Name: _____   Date: _____

During our visit to the Lyon School Outdoor Science Center, we observed several different gardens. Some of the things we noticed were pretty flowers, weeds, dead plants, vegetables, and damaged plants. Look at your garden or one in your neighborhood. Check what you see. Bring this checklist to school on Monday.

	YES	NO
1. tomatoes		
2. green beans		
3. pumpkins		
4. cucumbers		
5. squash		
6. corn		
7. flowers		
8. bees		
9. worms		
10. weeds		

How would you describe this garden? How does it compare to our school gardens?

_____

_____

_____

Figure 4.13

SOURCE: Used with permission from Jan Kirch and Debbie Shefren.

GARDEN SURVEY

Name: _____   Date: _____

Do you have a garden? _____

Why or why not? _____

_____

If you have a garden, what kind of garden is it? _____

_____

How did you decide what to put in your garden? _____

_____

_____

What is in your garden? _____

_____

Do you have a problem with your garden? Explain. _____

_____

Did you solve it? _____ How? _____

_____

What do you like about your garden? _____

_____

Thank you. Please return to your teacher.

Figure 4.14

SOURCE: Used with permission from Jan Kirch and Debbie Shefren.

To Reflect

1. How do the ideas presented in Chapter 4 relate to your teaching experiences? What ideas support and confirm what you are already doing?

2. What did you find in this chapter that you can share with colleagues? Did something suggest new possibilities for your program?

3. What questions does this chapter raise for further discussion and reflection?

_____ **Coming Next** _____

Working Together at the School Level

A Schoolwide Commitment to Literacy

Beginning a Dialogue About Literacy
Partnering With the School Library Media Specialist

Restoring the Joy of Reading

Celebrate Special Days

Coming Together to Celebrate Literacy: Annual Literature Festival
Principal Models Bedtime Story Reading

Coming Together to Create a Community of Readers: A Book Buffet
Book Collections
Magazine Exchange
Book Exchanges
Donations to School Libraries
Holiday Gift Suggestions
School Book Fairs and Bookstores
Author Visits to a School

Multitiered Model for Reading Support
Children Needing More Practice Reading

Coming Together to Bring Authors and Readers Together: Awesome
Authors and Dewey Elementary
Students Needing Help With Skill and Strategy Development
Providing Intensive Support at the Primary Level
Focused Instruction for Middle School Students: Tall Friends
Coordinating Strategies

School-Based Reading Labs for the Most Needy Readers

To Reflect

Working Together at the School Level

A SCHOOLWIDE COMMITMENT TO LITERACY

Our schools can make a tremendous difference in how children value literacy. Walk into some schools and immediately you know that reading and learning are important. In others the commitments are not so apparent. If we want to support all children in joining together to be part of the social fabric of a literate school, there is much we can do. The examples and suggestions in this chapter for ways to create cross-age and all-school literacy are included to help teachers working with the whole school find support for individual literacy efforts. They may also help create some new visions of additional ways schools can work together to stimulate greater engagement in literacy.

We cannot do everything, but often some reenergized attention to reading together can be special. Particularly in this era of accountability and testing, it is important to maintain a balance in activities so students will want to become active engaged readers. Recent reports have documented a decline in students' voluntary reading after the primary grades. According to a national survey "Kids and Family Reading Report" conducted by Scholastic (2006) about 40% of kids between the ages of five and eight are high-frequency readers (reading for fun every day); only 29% of kids ages 9–11 years old are high-frequency readers, and the percentage continues to decline through age 17. The study also reported a high correlation between children's frequency of reading and their parents' reading habits. An encouraging part of this survey was that 74%

of the parents said they valued reading for their children. Children, too, reported finding reading enjoyable and important, although boys had less positive attitudes toward reading than did girls. Parents and schools need to be self-conscious about nurturing children's reading habits so they will choose to read regularly. If schools become too task oriented and focus on the small pieces of reading all the time, we can lose sight of one of the most important goals: maintaining reading as a life long habit.

School professional teams can create an all-school commitment to making literacy enjoyable, a part of the school community, and visible for all those associated with the school. There are many ways this can happen.

BEGINNING A DIALOGUE ABOUT LITERACY

It is necessary to put energy into making reading more socially shared in your school. Conducting a survey can create a point of opening dialogue for the community. We did this across several schools and found interesting results that challenged teachers and school instructional support staff to make the need for visible literacy clear (see Figure 5.1). In some cases, intermediate teachers were particularly unaware that students did not think of them, the teachers, as readers. Librarians also rethought their roles as readers for upper level students. In one school the survey reminded teachers that community members and parents should be invited in to read favorite poems and articles with children as a way of making clear the importance of reading to adults. Too often the reading adults do occurs after children are in bed or in places that are not observed by children.

Why Focus Beyond the Classroom?

Actually, there are many ways working in the larger context of the school can be valuable.

- Older students are powerful role models for younger ones. Even more than teachers, they establish the norms for the younger students both in elementary and upper levels.

- Adults in the school community serve as role models for children. They need to know that adults value reading and participate in many kinds of reading on a regular basis.

- Shared events within a school provide a great deal of positive energy since most students like ways to show their accomplishments.

- Some activities (like book fairs and author visits) are only feasible when a school works together to provide a large pool of attendees.

- Students like to work together and help one another. Cross-age events have become great ways to stimulate more interest in literacy in older students.

- Special school events are memorable experiences that are savored sometimes for a lifetime.

- With the pressure on students to achieve on high-stakes and regular tests, there needs to be a balance so the joy of reading is not totally overshadowed.

- Teachers need to have opportunities to reaffirm the joy and fun of teaching and learning with one another and with the whole school community. Laughing and celebrating together provides needed energy.

This same survey can be used as a model for secondary students too. They generally want to modify it to make it more personal for their own questions. Some enjoy interviewing community members to elicit their perceptions of reading. Even without a survey, students can become more reflective observers of their environments. For example, one teacher asked his students to do an observational study of what people read during one day. Students observed before school, during the school day, and in the afterschool hours and recorded any instances when they saw people reading. They were amazed when they compiled the results. Reading started early, they learned. In the morning, they saw professionals reading newspapers as they waited for the commuter trains to take them to work. They watched people read the computerized screens in the bank window indicating the stock market changes and the automatic teller machines as they extracted money. The list went on and on and impressed the students with the wide range of reading behaviors engaged in throughout the day.

Another teacher had students focus their attention on reading to on-the-job reading. During the year, students visited different work places to assess literacy needs. The students again were amazed by the constant uses of reading for work. Infused with reading words were icons and computer symbols, so the students then got into a discussion of what kinds of printed signs really counted as reading. Could pictures and graphic displays count?

Partnering With the School Library Media Specialist

One of the most important partners in developing a school wide focus on literacy is the school library media specialist. While many schools are not fortunate enough to have full-time trained personnel in the library, most do have someone who is committed to this role, perhaps a teacher

Survey of Readers

Name _____

1. When you think of someone who is a reader, who do you think of? Give the person's name and relation to you, and explain what makes you think of this person as a reader.

2. Circle the things you see this person reading:

   - magazines
   - newspapers
   - comics
   - games
   - computer books

   - letters
   - cookbooks
   - manuals
   - e-mail
   - other _____

3. Where do you see this person reading?

4. Do your best friends read? _____ If you answered "Yes," how do you know?

5. Does your teacher like to read? _____ How do you know?

6. Do you have a school librarian or media specialist? Does this person like to read? How do you know?

7. Are you a reader? What kinds of things do you like to read?

8. Who helps you find good books and other material to read?

9. Does anyone read to you? _____ Do you or would you like to be read to? _____

10. What is the best thing about reading?

11. What kinds of materials should teachers help students learn to read? (e.g., magazines, newspapers, poetry, Web sites, music, books, letters, instructional manuals)

12. Do you read to anyone else? Tell about it and how often you read with them.

13. Does your principal like to read? How do you know?

14. Write anything here that will help us understand more about readers you know.

Figure 5.1

librarian. Library media personnel often provide essential leadership in promoting reading and developing children's joy of reading. They characterize their role as that of motivating learners to become readers and of cultivating learning more generally (Gordon as cited in Bush, 2005). Think of the varied ways they influence literacy in your school: It might be useful to have a discussion with the school librarian and make a list of the ways your school team perceives the role of the library in promoting reading. You might have a more in-depth discussion of possibilities for your school using Bush's book, *The School Buddy System: The Practice of Collaboration* (2003). Sometimes teachers are surprised by just how much librarians want to and can do to support literacy. Included in your list may be some of the following:

1. *Developing a collection of books and media that support both students' independent reading and their investigations of content materials.* Librarians generally subscribe to journals that review current books and materials as they are published. They augment the school collection based on their professional knowledge of what is good for children to read and what reflects their interests. The size of the circulation of a library collection is a good indicator of how successful the school is in providing an inviting collection for student use.

The library is also the place with the largest collection of informational books, magazines and reference materials and media. The importance of this specific focus has been enhanced by the use of the term "information literacy." Beyond being motivated to want to read, students also need to know how to use materials for learning. The beginning point is having good resources available. When teachers collaborate with the librarian, they can ensure that the books they need for their instructional programs are available. Teachers need to inform the school librarian of the curriculum topics that are covered in the curriculum, the kinds of projects students are asked to complete, and the way the library book and media collection can support classroom learning. When there is an open and ongoing dialogue, better resources can be provided. The more teachers and librarians plan in advance together, the more likely it is that the resources will be available. Having a wide range of materials and media can be especially important given the wide range of reading levels and experiences of children in any grade. The more there are materials at multiple reading levels and a variety of types of resources available, from print to artifacts, to media and electronic resources, the more students will be able to pursue their own interests and engage in their own research.

2. *Teaching students the skills needed to engage in inquiry and use information sources effectively.* Schools with library media specialists who work closely with the curriculum can ensure that students develop an increasingly sophisticated set of informational literacy skills. They learn how materials are organized in libraries, so they can be accessed easily. They are introduced to the variety of collections of resources that can be accessed—both physically and electronically. They learn how to frame questions, search using key descriptors, make notes of ideas and information with references included, evaluate sources of information, check information in other forms, synthesize what they learn, and present findings in interesting and varied ways for particular audiences.

3. *Coordinating the use of the World Wide Web and instructing students in how to use it effectively.* The electronic resources now available are staggering. Library media specialists can evaluate potential sources and put together Web collections and help teachers create Web quests for students. They can be partners with classroom teachers in developing the resources and in guiding students as they use them. Because there are skills needed for navigating the Web as a learning tool the library media person often coordinates the curriculum for this form of literacy. It can ensure that all students are guided in their use of the World Wide Web.

4. *Promoting and advocating good books.* Many library media specialists provide book talks in classrooms for students. I remember my first year of teaching when the librarian saved my independent reading program by bringing in a cart of books every time I began a new unit and doing book talks until the students found just the right book to engage them in learning about the topic under study. As a new teacher, I had very little knowledge of what books my students could read or what would capture their interests. The librarian was a lifesaver for my desire to increase the amount of reading my students did.

With the increasing numbers of children from other cultures in our schools, there is a need to find materials that reflect their experiences and backgrounds. Schools can showcase the diverse countries and communities from which children come by putting books and artifacts in the entry book cases, creating collections in the library, and bringing famous authors and stories to the school's attention. There is no better person to make this possible than the library media specialist working with classroom teachers and parents.

5. *Collaborating with classroom teachers as students engage in literary projects and inquiry.* As teachers provide more differentiated instruction in their classrooms and involve students in small group book clubs and

author studies, involving librarians is natural. They can help find good sets of books on the same theme, provide book talks and help in individual students' selection, and participate as observers in ongoing book discussions. When students read at very different levels, it can be helpful to have a second adult working with the students so the teacher can focus more attention on those students needing strong support.

Inquiry projects often flow between the classroom and library as students search for information and resources that answer their questions. Computers in the library can be helpful as many children are involved at the same time. With their knowledge of the range of resources available, librarians are often indispensable guides for children's research efforts. They can also dialogue with individual children to help them think through their ideas, the information they peruse, and articulate more of what it means.

RESTORING THE JOY OF READING

Celebrating the joy of reading is certainly a goal of teachers and schools. Students who love to read will read more and gain the riches that come from reading. Sharing the satisfaction corporately can also help students identify more with books and reading. Special events can also invite the less convinced readers to become more personally involved and assume more of a reader stance.

Schools can create exciting shared literacy events that make the joy of reading apparent to a whole community. One example of such an all-school literacy event was one in which all classrooms took part in the celebration of books. The culmination was an open house with all children sharing their favorite characters and books. Teachers helped children decide on their favorite characters from books they had been reading. Then the children planned how to dress as those characters, and with the help of the school and their families, they made costumes to represent them. At the same time, the children wrote notes for themselves on how they would introduce themselves as their character and reviewed their book to be sure they would tell as much as they could about their character. The children knew that they would be taking on the role of their character when other classes visited their room; and that when the parents came, they would want to engage in conversations with adults as their chosen character. Each character kept a copy of the book from which he or she came so once identified, the connection between the character and the text could be easily made.

The teachers were careful to talk with the students at length before they made their selections since they wanted the event to be successful for all, and some hasty choices might not be easy to represent nor have enough depth to be engaging. Some children who had special interests, especially in animals and nonfiction, had to be helped to think through ways to represent their characters. Biography turned out to be an easy choice since the real-life content made communication more direct.

Teachers too participated in the event, dressing up like their favorite characters from children's literature. There was discussion of taking on adult book characters, but the teachers wanted the children to be able to identify them easily and so chose to be part of the children's world.

When everyone was ready, the classes took turns inviting others into their room. The children would be dressed as their characters and introduce themselves to the guests. They would tell their names and where they were from (time and place) and explain a little about their lives. Other classes were prompted to ask questions of the characters to find out more about how they had solved their life problems, what they were doing next, and so on. This was not as easy as it sounded, and the teachers learned that this event was a perfect context for them to teach social skills of engaging in conversations. Everyone had to learn to introduce themselves to new people and had to learn to ask questions and engage in conversations.

The culmination of the favorite character event was the open house for parents and adults in the community. What a scene the library and gym became! To read more about how this project has evolved over the years, see the Coming Together to Celebrate Literacy.

CELEBRATE SPECIAL DAYS

Black History Month, Women's History Week, or International Literacy Day are other all-school focusing events that schools have engaged in to make literacy visible and to provide a theme that everyone can share in. Some schools have recently done a focus on family favorites (Our Families' Celebration) so all children and parents can share books from their culture and family life. Figure 5.2 provides a list of some special events around which schools have planned literacy activities. Coming Together to Create Literacy spotlights ideas of how schools can use a special day to create a focus on reading.

Special Events Calendar

September

Hispanic Heritage Month

National Book Festival

www.loc.gov/bookfest

International Literacy Day sponsored by the IRA

Hispanic American Read-In Chain sponsored by IRA and NCTE

National Book Week sponsored by the American Library Association

October

Teen Read Week sponsored by the Young Adult Library Services

Association (YALSA)

www.ala.org/teenread/

February

Black History Month

African American Read-In Chain by National Council of Teachers of English (NCTE) and International Reading Association (IRA)

National Caucus of the NCTE

www.ncte.org

International Reading Association

www.reading.org

March

National Women's History Month

www.nwhp.org

Dr. Seuss' Birthday (March 2)

www.nea.org

www.randomhouse.com/seussville/

April

National Children's Book Day

International Board on Books for Young People (IBBY)

www.usbby.org

May

Get Caught Reading Month

www.getcaughtreading.org

Figure 5.2

Coming Together to Celebrate Literacy

Annual Literature Festival

—Nancy Merel

For the past several years, our school has held annual literature festivals. The festivals are the finest examples of students, teachers, administrators, parents, and community leaders working together. The festivals are glorious days when the resource center, hallways, and classrooms are transformed into other worlds and other times. Each year a different genre is featured as a study by the entire school.

Our first year focused on folktales, tall tales, and fairy tales. The library became a fairy castle. Historical fiction was the focus of our second festival. The resource center became a western town. Parent volunteers built a Conestoga wagon, large enough to seat an entire class for leisure reading activities.

On the day of the festival, our school community—adults and children alike—dress as characters reflecting the festival's genre. Students' multidisciplinary content skills were brought to bear in their preparation for and participation in the festival. Listening comprehension improved as students heard stories read by guest readers. Theater, puppet shows, and dramatic readings were prepared by students using both their prior knowledge of the genre and what they learned about the content as they prepared these staged productions.

All components of an exemplary reading program are enhanced through these festivals. Children compare and contrast versions of the literature; adapt stories for performance; write, respond to, and interpret text; and extend their reading through writing expository, narrative, and persuasive pieces.

The festival's chosen genre is extended by all teachers, including the special area teachers. For example, students danced courtly dances, such as the minuet, with the music teacher. The gym teacher built an obstacle course based on fairy tale characters and settings. During our western fest, both gym and music teachers featured line and square dancing, cowboy poetry and ballads, and Aaron Copland music. During the Greek mythology festival, each gym class participated in our own version of the Greek Olympics.

Our teaching staff and students are fortunate to enjoy language arts through many learning styles. Our school has studied and adapted the philosophy of Dr. Howard Gardner's multiple intelligences theory. We've used these intelligences in all curricular areas. We are proud of the authentic ways we have used literature. Building literacy for our school community is the cornerstone of building our learning environment.

Even when there is no other particular stimulus, you can create a focus on books by holding a book buffet or having students prepare a special lunch focused on food mentioned in books they have read. Once again, teachers are combining fun events: eating, reading, and special books. See Coming Together to Create a Community of Readers for a fun activity combining food and reading.

Principal Models Bedtime Story Reading

Parents also need to be reminded of the importance of continuing their involvement in their children's reading. By making bedtime reading a visible community event, the message is clear: Reading at home is a warm and enjoyable experience as well as an important one in the development of young readers.

Once or twice a year, Principal Judy Yturriago invites all of the students (kindergarten through fifth grade) in her school to come back in the evening to hear a bedtime story. Children gather in the library or the gym, wearing pajamas, nightgowns, and robes. Some even carry stuffed animals! The principal, wearing pajamas and big fluffy slippers, sits in a rocking chair and reads aloud for about an hour. Students enjoy the novelty of being in school dressed for bed, and the atmosphere is relaxed. Parents, too, enjoy the fun. They see how children love being read to and may recommit themselves to reading aloud at home.

Literary Genres That Can Be Used to Develop School Literature Festivals

- Bears in literature
- Biographies
- Children in literature
- Diaries
- Expository text
- Giants in literature
- Science fiction
- Teachers in literature

Coming Together to Create a Community of Readers

A Book Buffet

—*Joanne Ratliff*

Finding ways to create a community of readers can be challenging. Combining food with a love of books can expose readers to new books, encourage reading and sharing of books, and bond a group through the sharing of food.

Similar to a potluck dinner, a book buffet is held to develop fellowship and sharing. Each participant in a group is asked to bring a dish to share. The dish, however, has to connect to a book in some way. In my university classes, the book connection has to be to a children's book. I encourage students to be creative and not always go with the obvious (e.g., *If You Give a Mouse a Cookie*). Books are displayed with the dishes brought. Each participant is given a minute or two to explain the connection between their book and the food to be shared.

Books may have a personal connection for a particular participant that may not be readily apparent to the group. One student brought spaghetti and meatballs with the book *Carl's Birthday* by Alexandra Day. We were all curious about the connection until the student shared that her favorite food was spaghetti and meatballs. Her father, Carl, did not like this dish, but each year on her birthday she got to choose the dinner. So the connection was perfect. This example clarifies the need for the book connection sharing. Not only was the connection interesting, but the telling of it served to help build a caring community classroom. The connection can be direct (bringing spaghetti and meatballs to accompany *Cloudy With a Chance of Meatballs* or a relish tray with *Pickles to Pittsburgh*, both books are by Judi Barrett). For other clever connections, see Food for Thought below.

A variation of the book buffet is the poetry picnic. Instead of sharing a dish related to a book, students bring one related to a poem. Before eating, each participant reads or recites his or her poem.

Title Connections to Food

- *The Accidental Zucchini: An Unexpected Alphabet* by Max Grover
- *Bread, Bread, Bread* by Ann Morris
- *Chicken Sunday* by Patricia Polacco
- *The Lemon Drop Jar* by Christine Widman
- *The Little Red Hen Makes a Pizza* by Philemon Sturges
- *Pete's a Pizza* by William Steig

Making Connections With Ethnic Foods

- *A Birthday Basket for Tia* by Pat Mora
- *The Cajun Gingerbread Boy* by Berthe Amoss
- *Gaston Goes to Mardi Gras* by James Rice
- *A Grain of Rice* by Helena Carle Pittman
- *The King's Chessboard* by David Birch
- *Mama Provi and the Pot of Rice* by Sylvia Rosa-Casanova
- *Mimi's First Mardi Gras* by Alice Couvillon
- *On Mardi Gras Day* by Fatima Shaik
- *One Grain of Rice: A Mathematical Folktale* by Demi
- *The Seven Chinese Brothers* by Margaret Mahy
- *Too Many Tamales* and *Chato's Kitchen* by Gary Soto

General Food Connections

- *Pot Luck* by Tobi Tobias
- *Strega Nona* by Tomie de Paolo
- *The Very Hungry Caterpillar* by Eric Carle

In a school that is racially, culturally, and economically diverse—with many second language learners—bedtime story night is an opportunity for Dr. Yturriago to model the benefits of reading aloud to children. It is a night for students from all grades and from a variety of reading backgrounds to experience the pleasure of listening to a good story handled by the school librarians or parents' groups, with a percentage of the proceeds going back to the school.

Book Collections

Many schools collect canned goods and other food at Thanksgiving and the winter holidays to share with less fortunate people in the community. One nice variant is that the children add books to their donation boxes, so the feeding of body and spirit go hand in hand. There are lovely books about Thanksgiving that make a very appropriate addition to the sharing schools do. As the food is collected—often in the hallway of the school—an attractive display can include books about the historical reason for sharing at this time and about the holiday in general. We have found that with the addition of large numbers of immigrants to our country, the foundations of Thanksgiving are often unknown to some families in our community. Therefore, both for the school's families and those with whom the food is shared, attention to the origins and traditions associated with Thanksgiving is important. The same is true of the winter holiday sharing events. Children enjoy learning the meanings of Hanukkah, Christmas, and Kwanzaa. These can be shared by including books in whatever outreach the school makes at this time of year.

Magazine Exchange

One urban high school considered the kinds of materials available to students and realized that not only was there no bookstore in the area but also the families were not in the habit of buying newspapers or magazines. Therefore, the principal decided to create a magazine exchange program. Faculty and staff were encouraged to bring in their magazines (minus the mailing labels) after they had read them to donate them to the magazine box in the office area. Students were then encouraged to look through the magazines and select one per week to take home to read. The response was most encouraging. Students became aware of the wealth of available magazines that reflect a wide range of interests—from fashion to skateboarding to cars and sports as well as news and current affairs.

As the principal developed the idea for the magazine exchange, he decided that the receptacle for the magazines needed to be attractive, too. The result was a large box decorated with front pages of many magazines as an invitation to readers to come and browse. By having the box in the entry hall of the school, visitors became aware of the opportunity to recycle good magazines and the whole community participated.

Book Exchanges

Book exchanges are also a good way to encourage the sharing of books. If you are in an area where students buy paperback books, a periodical exchange can also be useful and enjoyable. It encourages transfer among the students of books without the cost of always purchasing new ones. These are usually student-to-student swaps rather than one-way donations. In these exchanges, students usually receive a ticket for each book brought in. Students then select another book or books they want to take and give their ticket or tickets for that book.

At Washington Elementary School in Evanston, Illinois, the PTA sponsors a book exchange program called Book Nook. Its goal is to provide an opportunity for every student in an economically diverse population to choose and own books. They may trade a book from home or buy one for less than fifty cents. To stock the program, the PTA collects used books through donations and local rummage and library sales. Every Tuesday, two parent volunteers set up rolling shelves of books in the main hall. During a two-hour period, each classroom teacher brings his or her students to visit the book nook during an assigned time. Students have 5 or 10 minutes to browse through the books and make a trade or purchase. Book nook is successful in several ways. It is fun for both students and parent volunteers. There is a lot of excited talk about which books are out each week and what to choose; children ask each other, the parent volunteers, and even passing teachers and other adults to recommend good reads. Many students try out a first chapter book at book nook, and others may enjoy picking out a book to take home to a younger sibling. It is a risk-free time to enjoy literacy on many levels.

Share the Wealth Establishing a Book Exchange

To establish a book exchange for a whole school or grade level, a more formal process is usually helpful. Designate a committee to be in charge and have them set ground rules so the process can move smoothly. A key consideration is finding an area where books can be collected and then displayed. Develop a letter for parents if you are in an elementary or middle school. Work with the PTA or parent volunteers to involve as many parents as seems appropriate. They can be invaluable in collecting the books and creating the actual exchange event.

Where students do not have many books of their own, you can contact publishers who have remaindered paperback books. They will sometimes donate these books for no charge if you pick them up. What they do is take off the front covers so the books cannot be resold, but they leave the books intact. These books can then be distributed to students or used as rewards for good achievement or school contributions. The idea is for students to have the opportunity to collect their own books to create their own personal libraries. Until students can possess a book, the value of such ownership eludes them.

Donations to School Libraries

As we prioritize the value of literacy, we can also help students think of books and magazines as gifts to give. We want our students to learn the value of giving books as gifts and build the foundation for a lifetime habit. We can help encourage them in the practice of thinking of books as gifts by making such gift giving part of the elementary school culture. Some teachers do this by suggesting that when children celebrate their birthdays with their class, they make a book donation to the school library. The teacher can help students create bookmarks that are inserted in the front of the book at the time it is donated, or they can buy commercial ones. These indicate who donated the book and the birthday on which it was given. Children can take great pride in the special books they select for the school library; I have seen children take their friends to the place where their special books are shelved and show off the bookmarks. Periodically the school librarian may also highlight these donations when doing a book talk or reading aloud to a group of students. The more the students think of the library as a part of themselves, something they can help develop, the more this valuable resource will become.

In schools where the financial resources of parents are limited, teachers may also make contributions to the library in the name of students who have made special accomplishments or who the teacher wants to recognize. Donating books as a memorial is one way to remember children or adults lost through tragedy or illness. In so many different ways it is possible to connect the ongoing events of the school with special book contributions that then create a real shared literacy. Such modeling can help parents begin to think more seriously about giving books for birthdays, holidays, and other special events.

Holiday Gift Suggestions

Holidays provide a natural opportunity for teachers to suggest the purchase of good books and magazine subscriptions for children. A team of teachers can prepare a list of recent books and give ordering information, so parents and family members can purchase them. (One easy source for books is Amazon.com.) A list of magazines for children and adolescents is available in the book *Magazines for Kids and Teens*, edited by Donald R. Stoll; purchasing information is included. Some schools have also sent home lists of good magazines for children just before holidays and as suggestions for birthday presents.

School Book Fairs and Bookstores

Access to books varies considerably from community to community. Some communities have bookstores where a wide selection of children's books is readily available. Other communities do not have good sources for the purchase of books. If you are interested in a discussion of the importance of access to books, you may want to read Susan Neuman et al.'s (2001) work on this important topic. Even if there are bookstores available, it may be a good idea to make the purchase of books even easier by bringing them into the school. The easiest way to do this is to hold an annual book sale with a local book distributor in charge of bringing the books into the school. A richer option, in terms of student learning, is for the students to develop and run their own bookstore and sell books weekly themselves. This option takes much more time and energy but can be most rewarding.

The fall is a good time to hold a book sale. Just before the holiday period, both parents and students can have a good time selecting books for themselves and for gifts to be given to others. The PTA or a volunteer group can be in charge of the event with proceeds going to the school. Someone needs to be the liaison from the faculty to ensure the kinds of books selected fit the reading interests and levels of the school. Ideas about themes and content covered in the curriculum can enhance the value of the purchases. The adults in charge can work with the local book distributor or bookstore representatives to make sure the books displayed fit the needs and interests of the school. Having a secure location for the book sale is also important. It takes a great deal of time and energy to set up the books, and the easier it is for a book distributor to have access to the space, the more likely they will bring a full range of materials and also return for another year. Usually a percentage of the revenues can be designated to return to the school for the purchase of books, and the book distributor should give a school discount as part of the original arrangements. If the sale is well advertised and is in a room that is accessible before and after school, the results can be exciting for everyone concerned. In our school the book sale has become an annual event, and everyone waits eagerly for this special time.

One group of local middle school students, with their teacher's encouragement, decided they wanted to run a bookstore themselves as part of an economics education project their teacher suggested. The students developed a survey to ascertain the interests of other students and to determine if they would be willing to purchase paperback books and to get an idea of how many each might buy. Developing, administering, and coding the survey was a big project in and of itself. However, that was just the beginning. The students also had to persuade the principal that there was a space for a small book nook that could be secured when not being used. Their idea of selling paper and pencils (a real issue for some teachers since many students seemed to come to school without those resources) made the bookstore appealing to teachers and led to the principal's approval. Then students had to contact publishers and distributors of books to persuade them that sending books on consignment would work. Space, book racks, and the logistics of collecting money and bookkeeping were all part of the planning process. The result was a visible and highly used paperback bookstore in the school. Yet, it took a great deal of time and reprioritized energy to make it work.

Author Visits to a School

Getting to know authors of the wonderful books written for children and adolescents is another way to make literacy come alive in the school. This is an opportunity for collaboration among teachers and the library media teacher or specialist. Planning a successful visit by an author takes careful planning; it is a time when many classes should be able to be actively involved. Initially, many teachers introduce students to authors through Web sites that give good background information about the authors as well as their responses to frequently asked questions. Since so many authors make themselves available to speak at conferences, teachers can hear authors speak and can bring back audiotapes of parts of their talks, autographed books, and descriptions of interesting moments with the authors. An overused way to make connections is to have students write to favorite authors. These letters may become required assignments, and the connection can lose the motivating intent—to connect with a real author—if not handled carefully. With the Web sites now available, the level of information most generally sought by students can be accessed more easily. But real letter exchanges are exciting and make writers come alive to students. Many authors come to cities to give talks at area bookstores and libraries too. Planning a visit to one of these events or sending a team of students can be exciting. Contact bookstores in your area and get a schedule of their special events with authors. Posting that list and keeping the possibilities real for students can introduce children to another way of meeting the authors of books they love to read. Teachers and students can have their interests in books sparked by these personal connections with writers.

The most exciting experience of all is, naturally, being able to have an author visit your own school. This is very possible since publishers are quite generous in making authors available to schools. The key to such visits is ensuring that the students have read many of the author's works and are interested in knowing more about the writer. The writer cannot be a favorite of the teachers only! Preparing for visits is essential. Students need to take time forming questions they want to ask the visiting author. Students can research author biographies to learn as much as possible about the author. The more specific and knowledgeable the students are, the better the exchanges can be. After forming good questions, students need to practice having an author as a guest in the room. Some rehearsal of protocol for adult guests shows respect to the visitors that come to the room, so practice in meeting guests and having hostesses and hosts for them will yield long-term benefits. Coming Together to Bring Authors and Readers Together details the Awesome Authors program, an ongoing project at Dewey School in Evanston, Illinois.

MULTITIERED MODEL FOR READING SUPPORT

Children in an environment where literacy is shared and savored also want to read well. Helping children improve their reading can be a schoolwide effort rather than one assigned solely to the classroom. Adult volunteers, other children, and support staff can all help provide the individual attention developing readers need. However, it is important that students receive the level of support they need to become more fluid and flexible readers. Some children simply need many opportunities to read in a warm and personal context. Others need specific help with underlying skills and strategies. Some students may need carefully orchestrated guided tutoring to overcome substantial problems with reading. Each level of need calls for different kinds of programs.

Children Needing More Practice Reading

There are a variety of ways schools can support readers who need to spend more time with books and magazines. Bringing in volunteers to sit and read with children is becoming a more common practice in schools around the country as a result of the America Reads program sponsored by the United States Department of Education. In this project college students can receive tuition credit to reduce their student loans by working in schools as reading tutors. Materials have been developed by the International Reading Association (IRA) (i.e., *Volunteer Tutor Handbook*, 1998) to help tutors become skilled resources for schools to use to help struggling readers. The project has led many schools to explore ways to provide more one-on-one time for children to read with older readers. Parents can come into the classrooms to read with certain children on an individual basis. All a parent volunteer or the teacher has to do is list times when adults are available to come to the classroom, make a list of students who will benefit by the practice, and match them together. The teacher's responsibility is to make sure the students are ready with reading materials when the volunteer reading partners arrive and that there is a semiprivate space to use. Schools near senior citizen centers have found that retirees (grandparent surrogates) often are delighted to serve as reading partners for elementary students. Senior citizen volunteers may come to the school or the children can walk to the center if near enough. These cross-generational relationships can be effective on many levels.

Some schools also use older children as reading buddies for younger readers. The upper grade students come to the primary classrooms or meet in the library and listen to the children read to them on a periodic basis. The more regularly the students meet with their buddies, the better the project works since they can develop a friendship and connection with more contact. Some buddy programs have the older students also reading to their younger partners periodically. In this way, the older children share their own interests and special books, and the younger children hear the language of books that stretch them to a higher level. Older students model what a good developing reader sounds like, so the younger students can build their own expectation for their reading.

Teachers have created this very popular and successful cross-age reading program they call Little Buddies. At the beginning of the year, each fifth grade student is assigned a little buddy from the kindergarten class. For about half an hour each week, these big and little buddies meet to talk, play quietly, and, especially, to read. The fifth graders might read aloud books that their kindergarten friends have chosen, and the younger students might practice new reading skills. For both groups, it is a time of sharing, learning, and bonding.

COMING TOGETHER TO BRING
AUTHORS AND READERS TOGETHER

Awesome Authors and Dewey Elementary

At Dewey Elementary School in Evanston, Illinois, a group of parents interested in literacy formed a PTA committee called Awesome Authors. Each fall, the committee chooses three children's authors or author-illustrators to highlight in various ways throughout the year. The PTA provides funds to purchase the authors' books. Teachers receive book lists for each author and, along with the school librarian, encourage students to read them. Some teachers choose to read many of the books aloud in class, and each year's Awesome Authors books are prominently displayed in the library. Once students have read four books by one author, they are invited to join Fun Lunch, a group led during lunch periods by a parent volunteer. At Fun Lunch, students participate in an activity related to the author's work. For example, when students had read Ed Young's version of *Sadako and the Thousand Paper Cranes*, they learned to make origami cranes. As a culminating event, the Awesome Authors committee tries to schedule one of the authors to visit the school and meet with students. During one very special year, author-illustrator Patricia Pallaco came. In anticipation of her visit, teachers, parents, and children worked together to greet the author with an array of illustrations they had created in Pallaco's style. Students were thrilled to meet a person they had spent the year getting to know through her books and pictures.

Students Needing Help With Skill and Strategy Development

Many students seem to miss some of the underlying skills and strategies needed to be good readers. To help them develop these skills and strategies, focused instruction is important. This requires trained tutors working under the guidance of a teacher or reading specialist. Three very different ways of providing this added instruction may help you think creatively about how such help can be found in your school.

Providing Intensive Support at the Primary Level

Pat Cunningham and Dottie Hall developed the four blocks program, a model for intensive support for primary students by using teams of teacher specialists who together come into one classroom at a time and provide added instructional support. The reading specialist, the special education teacher, the speech and hearing specialist, and other specialists in the school become a support team. They develop a regular schedule of visits to classrooms and spend half an hour a day in each room. During that time they work with small groups of students under the teacher's guidance. They can reinforce skills and strategies the teacher has already introduced or serve as teachers for small groups of students. Students receive intensive instruction in a small, intimate setting, and the trained specialists can monitor and adjust instruction to fit the students' developing abilities.

Focused Instruction for Middle School Students: Tall Friends

At MacArthur Middle School in Prospect Heights, Illinois, reading specialist Mary Ann Duderstadt (Allen, 2000), who taught remedial reading for 28 years, developed a tutoring program called "Tall Friends." This program helps two groups of readers. Middle school students who come to

Dutterstead for reading remediation receive focused instruction for their reading needs and also become tutors for primary children who need help in reading. This program supports both levels of students. Each day during summer school, the seventh and eighth graders come for the full morning. During the first two hours they work on their own reading needs. During the next hour and a half, these middle graders turn their focus to the primary students they tutor. They learn to help students understand the basics of language by working on phonic elements with word sort activities, creating sentences, and many other manipulative activities. In this process, the older students also become more proficient with the basic decoding skills. The tutors keep a record of their teaching in a daily journal. These journals are given to the primary students' teachers in the fall. The tutors also write a two-page reflection on what they learned about themselves and their students, which includes documentation with specific examples from the students' work. Each summer, 15 students will tutor up to 45 primary children. The success of this program in raising the reading levels of the students and increasing their self-esteem has led Dutterstead to extend the program now to the regular school year. Students work after school with the primary children in similar supervised ways to boost their reading development.

Coordinating Strategies

A third way schools have worked across grade levels is to develop a set of strategies that teachers all emphasize at the same time (Ogle & Hunter, 2001). This is especially useful when students are with more than one teacher a day. Teachers put posters with the strategy of the week or month clearly highlighted in their rooms. Whenever possible they model for students using this strategy. Students who are known to need more help get special attention. Sometimes it is by partnering them with another classmate. Sometimes it is by having a support person sit with them as they read to encourage and support their use of the strategy. Sometimes it is by having the special reading teacher work in the room to coach the students needing help. We have seen real progress made by students who finally make the connection between what they are taught about reading and the ways to apply those strategies in their ongoing reading.

SCHOOL-BASED READING LABS FOR THE MOST NEEDY READERS

Some students need intensive help with reading. When they are significantly lower in their levels of reading from most other students, providing

concentrated instruction under the guidance of trained reading specialists is important. Some students at all grade levels need this support.
Results from early reading intervention programs, particularly Reading
Recovery, have been able to demonstrate the importance of having highly
trained specialists work with the most needy students. Programs for students
in higher grades are also needed yet not as frequently developed. Many
times parents end up taking their children to private tutoring programs to
augment what is not being done at school. It is much better if a special
reading program is available within the school itself to help these developing readers. Schools that do provide help for such students do so in several
different ways. Special reading teachers may take small groups of
students for intensive instruction for short periods of time and work with
them either in the classroom or in a separate setting. In some cases, the
specialists work with these students before a unit of instruction begins in
the regular classroom to jump-start their learning. Preliminary instruction, helping students focus on the topic or theme, teaching pertinent
vocabulary and word elements, having students read materials in advance,
and scaffolding assignments, can make successful classroom participation
possible for many students.

In other cases, students need continued instruction that is at a different level and focus than that provided in the classroom. Schools can either
structure an extended day so students have double the reading instruction
they would otherwise get, or they can adjust some aspect of the curriculum so more reading time is made available. Some schools also provide
weekend and summer instructional support so students have added time
for learning under carefully guided support. Other schools have linked up
with universities and brought pre-service teachers into the school to help
provide more individual instruction. The reading specialist may prepare
the lesson plans for these pre-service teachers to use so there is continuity
in the instructional focus the students receive.

Middle and high schools often have reading teachers who meet with
students who need continued reading instruction in special reading
classes. These classes have many different formats, some being individual-
ized labs, some organized around literature discussion, and others with
more traditional teacher-directed lessons and guided reading (Ogle, 2006).
The use of computers has made it possible to provide a greater variety of
activities and materials. Students who are new to this country can begin
to learn the distinguishing phonemes and orthographic system of English
on computers and can listen repeatedly to some appropriate oral text reading, clicking on words that are unfamiliar. Students with comprehension
problems can be working with problem-solving programs like the GLOBE

network (Kennedy & Canney, 2001, pp. 310–329); other students can be writing responses to their reading or communicating with students in other schools, and others can be creating graphic summaries using Inspiration software. Reading centers for these students should be as inviting as any classroom in the school. They need the most support in building positive associations with reading. High-interest materials, magazines and newspapers, and print that they identify with are all important. So is having comfortable places to relax and read!

Since students needing added reading instruction are found in all teachers' classrooms, providing support at a schoolwide level is important. We cannot let students passively underachieve in reading. Every effort must be made to ensure that all students receive appropriate reading instruction and that those farther behind can accelerate their progress so that they will become competent readers able to function independently in their classes and outside of school.

Meeting the developmental reading needs of all our students is a challenge since the better they are taught, the wider will be their abilities and interests. For example, gifted students are often not challenged as much as they should be. With more specific instruction for all students, the best should become even more proficient as all students improve and a wider range of achievement results (Organisation for Economic Co-operation and Development [OECD], 2001). The good news is that with increased attention to high standards at the state and district levels, more support focused on instruction in reading is being provided. Chapter 6 describes some of these resources.

To Reflect

1. How do the ideas presented in Chapter 5 relate to your teaching experiences? What ideas support and confirm what you are already doing?

2. What did you find in this chapter that you can share with colleagues? Did something suggest new possibilities for your program?

3. What questions does this chapter raise for further discussion and reflection?

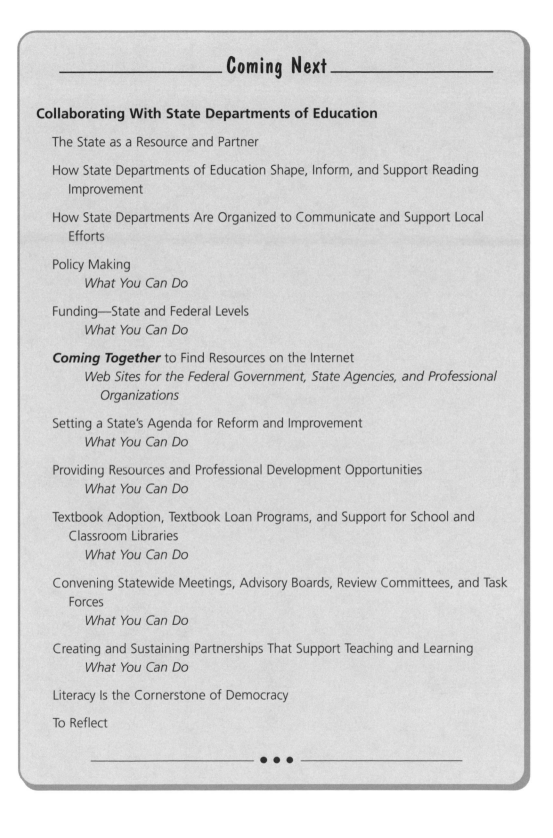

_____ **Coming Next** _____

Collaborating With State Departments of Education

The State as a Resource and Partner

How State Departments of Education Shape, Inform, and Support Reading
Improvement

How State Departments Are Organized to Communicate and Support Local
Efforts

Policy Making
What You Can Do

Funding—State and Federal Levels
What You Can Do

Coming Together to Find Resources on the Internet
*Web Sites for the Federal Government, State Agencies, and Professional
Organizations*

Setting a State's Agenda for Reform and Improvement
What You Can Do

Providing Resources and Professional Development Opportunities
What You Can Do

Textbook Adoption, Textbook Loan Programs, and Support for School and
Classroom Libraries
What You Can Do

Convening Statewide Meetings, Advisory Boards, Review Committees, and Task
Forces
What You Can Do

Creating and Sustaining Partnerships That Support Teaching and Learning
What You Can Do

Literacy Is the Cornerstone of Democracy

To Reflect

Collaborating With State Departments of Education

THE STATE AS A RESOURCE AND PARTNER

We all know that to be teachers we need to be certified by our state department of education. But that is just the beginning of the state involvement in our teaching. It is at the state level that many important decisions and directions that shape our teaching are determined. As we think about the educational community of which we are a part, we need to include our state level educational agencies and begin to see ourselves as active participants in the state level activities. We are very fortunate to be teaching at a time when there is support for education at the state level. We also know that without our active involvement, decision makers may lack important input in setting policy and direction. The experience in some states should warn us that we cannot ignore the structures and people who are designated to promote education throughout the state. It is not a luxury for us to become acquainted with our state agencies—it is essential. It is through them that many of the resources for materials, textbooks, staff development, and special programs are made available.

I could think of no better way to explore the various levels of activity and resources provided by our state agencies than to have someone who has worked at the State Board of Education for a number of years explain this important part of our network. Thanks to Dr. Eunice Greer, former division administrator of Illinois, who has contributed this chapter.

HOW STATE DEPARTMENTS OF EDUCATION SHAPE, INFORM, AND SUPPORT READING IMPROVEMENT

State departments of education can be tremendous resources and can play important leadership roles in the reading improvement process. Educators will benefit most from these state department activities when they are informed about the following:

- how their state departments are organized,
- how policies are made and implemented,
- how funding is determined and allocated,
- how initiatives are created and implemented,
- how to access resources, and
- how to contribute to the design and development process.

HOW STATE DEPARTMENTS ARE ORGANIZED TO COMMUNICATE AND SUPPORT LOCAL EFFORTS

It is true that state departments of education vary in terms of the services they provide. But typically, state systems of public education are organized around a multitiered leadership and governance model. Many of them look something like Figure 6.1.

A common misconception is that state departments of education make the laws that govern local schools. I often hear local educators criticize a new piece of legislation and attribute its creation to their state department of education. State departments of education are not charged with legislative powers. Typically, their role and responsibility in a state government is to craft the rules and regulations to implement new and amended legislation once it has passed out of the legislature and has been signed into law. So it is really more accurate to say that state departments of education inform policy making and implement legislation.

POLICY MAKING

As stated above, state departments of education do not make or pass laws. They can work to inform legislators during the lawmaking process. Often state department staff will solicit testimonial support from local administrators and educators. Sometimes local educators will be invited to testify before House or Senate subcommittees during hearings on pending legislation. Once new laws have been passed or old legislation has been

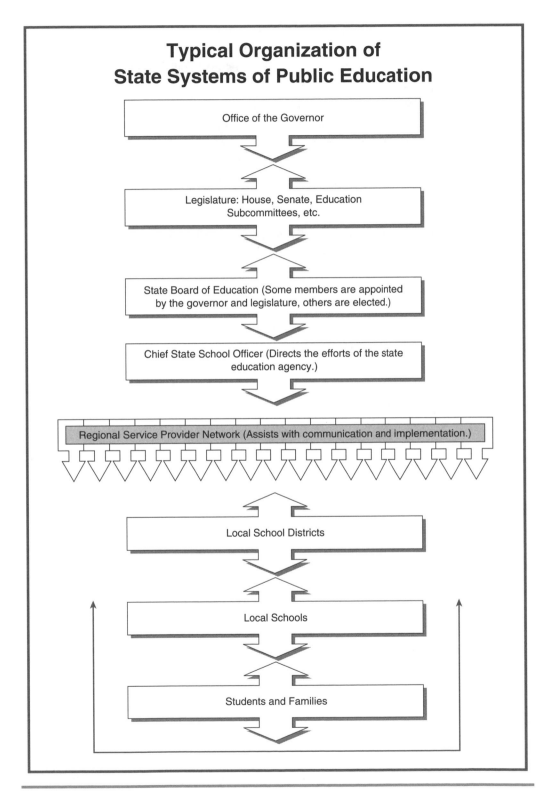

Typical Organization of State Systems of Public Education

Office of the Governor

Legislature: House, Senate, Education Subcommittees, etc.

State Board of Education (Some members are appointed by the governor and legislature, others are elected.)

Chief State School Officer (Directs the efforts of the state education agency.)

Regional Service Provider Network (Assists with communication and implementation.)

Local School Districts

Local Schools

Students and Families

Figure 6.1

amended, state departments of education work to translate new laws and amendments into school code, guidelines, and rules and regulations. In many states, the drafting of new rules and regulations will be informed by regional focus groups, public hearings, and other means of soliciting public review and comment. When new rules and regulations are written, there is usually a window of time that is dedicated to building public awareness and to notifying all affected school personnel of how the new rules and regulations will impact their jobs. If there are any new expectations for things like reporting information, testing students, funding programs, credentialing professionals, or determining eligibility for programs, the forms, procedures, and protocols for implementation are put in place during this window of time. Whenever possible, a great deal of time and energy is devoted to creating awareness and ensuring that everyone impacted by new rules and regulations has been notified and is prepared to implement the new language. The complexity of the new legislation and policies being implemented determines how much time will be devoted to preparing for implementation and creating public awareness. A state may devote up to two years' time to prepare its school population for a newly mandated assessment. A state may spend as little as a month to notify administrative offices of a change in the equation appearing on a particular form schools are required to use to report building or district level data to the state.

What You Can Do

We desperately need to increase legislators' awareness of factors that affect our efforts to improve teaching and learning. Traditionally, legislators are not educators. They come out of courtrooms, boardrooms, and corporate offices and occasionally from pulpits, town halls, and squad cars. Rarely do they come out of our classrooms. They are not experts in education. They bring to their lawmaking activities very little knowledge of how schools work, what teachers and administrators do, how children learn, what schools need, or what works. If we want our lawmakers to represent our needs and interests well, we need to tell them! They are likely to work with more than 2,000 pieces of pending legislation in any one session. If we want them to pay attention to issues on education and schooling, we need to get their attention, show them the evidence that what we want is sound and good practice for our children, and be clear and succinct about how the new legislation can or cannot contribute to improved performances in schools throughout the state. We are in no position to criticize and condemn new legislative agendas and laws unless we take an active role in informing and shaping our legislators' thinking on the issues. Look for public hearings, focus groups, and town meetings. Organize letter writing, e-mail, and phone campaigns.

Do you know the names, street and e-mail addresses, and phone numbers of your state and federal representatives and senators? Make it a point to visit your state's Web site and get this information. Post it in your teachers' lounge or workroom. If your school or PTA sends out newsletters during the year, add these people to your mailing list. Ask to be added to their constituent mailing lists, too. If you go to your local newspaper with your students' accomplishments, send each of your state legislators a copy of the article. If your school is having a special event or an open house, send invitations to your state legislators. Create awareness so that you can begin to build a relationship and so that they begin to identify you as a source of information, support, and expertise.

FUNDING—STATE AND FEDERAL LEVELS

All public schools are funded with a combination of local, state, and federal dollars. Complex funding formulas are used to compute per-pupil expenditures and as support for free and reduced lunch programs, Title I allocations, and a host of other funding streams that support school programs. In addition to these, state departments also oversee the awarding of competitive state and federal grant funds to schools. Most recently, federal grant programs have included the Reading Excellence Act grant awards, the Comprehensive School Reform funds, and the upcoming Reading First program. Typically, state departments of education will announce these programs to local schools and districts, sponsor informational publications and workshops, conduct competitions, review local proposals for funds, award grants, and monitor and evaluate implementation of the funding.

What You Can Do

In the past five or six years, data-driven and research-based decision making have provided the framework for federal grant awards in education. Proposal writing guidelines make it clear that funds will be awarded based in part on evidentiary data and a research-based rationale for implementation. This new focus challenges educators to do several things.

First, make a commitment to work to bring more grant money into your school or district. Identify a leadership team that will coordinate grant writing efforts. Monitor state and federal Web sites that post grant announcements and call for proposals. (See Coming Together to Find Resources on the Internet for a list of important Web sites.) Identify grant opportunities that match your school's or district's agendas, vision, and goals and share them with your local leadership team.

Second, if you are not already reading the research in your field of interest, you need to begin. There are several recent publications that will get you started, and a membership in a national professional organization like the International Reading Association (IRA), the National Council of Teachers of English (NCTE), or the National Association for the Education of Young Children (NAEYC) will provide you with ongoing access to current research. Knowledge of current, relevant research is a key element of a successful grant proposal. Consider beginning a study team in your school so that you and your colleagues can learn together, build a common knowledge base that informs your practice, and share ideas and new learning.

Coming Together to Find Resources on the Internet

Web Sites for the Federal Government, State Agencies, and Professional Organizations

American Library Association (ALA)
http://www.ala.org/

America Reads
http://www.ed.gov/inits/americareads/

Association for Supervision and Curriculum Development (ASCD)
http://www.ascd.org/

Between the Lions
http://pbskids.org/lions/

Book Adventure
http://www.bookadventure.com/

Bulletin of the Center for Children's Books
http://www.lis.uiuc.edu/puboff/bccb/

Center for Children's Books
http://www.lis.uiuc.edu/~ccb/

Center for the Book in the Library of Congress
http://www.loc.gov/loc/cfbook/

Center for the Improvement of Early Reading Achievement (CIERA)
http://www.ciera.org/

Children's Book Council (CBC)
http://www.cbcbooks.org/

Children's Literacy Initiative (CLI)
http://www.cliontheweb.org/

Council for Exceptional Children (CEC)
http://www.cec.sped.org/

Council of Chief State School Officers (CCSSO)
http://www.ccsso.org/

Electronic Classroom
http://www.readingonline.org/electronic/elec_index.asp

International Reading Association (IRA)
http://www.reading.org/

Links of Interest to Students and Teachers of English as a Second Language
http://www.aitech.ac.jp/~iteslj/links/

National Assessment of Educational Progress (NAEP)
http://www.nces.ed.gov/nationsreportcard/

National Association for the Education of Young Children (NAEYC)
http://www.naeyc.org/

National Center for Family Literacy (NCFL)
http://www.famlit.org/

National Center for Learning Disabilities (NCLD)
http://www.ld.org/

National Clearinghouse for Bilingual Education (NCBE)
http://www.ncbe.gwu.edu/

National Council of Teachers of English
http://www.ncte.org/

National Institute for Literacy (NIFL)
http://www.nifl.gov/

National Institute of Child Health and Human Development (NICHD)
http://www.nichd.nih.gov/

National Reading Panel (NRP)
http://www.nationalreadingpanel.org/

National Research Center on English Learning and Achievement (CELA)
http://cela.albany.edu/

National Writing Project (NWP)
http://www.writingproject.org/

PBS Literacy Link
http://www.pbs.org/literacy/

Reading Is Fundamental (RIF)
http://www.rif.org/

Third, collect and store data to document classroom, building, and district level reading improvement efforts. Carefully document the implementation and impact of research-based practices. Almost every new call for proposals asks for data to support requests for new funds.

SETTING A STATE'S AGENDA FOR REFORM AND IMPROVEMENT

The forces that set or change a state's agenda for reform and improvement are most often complex and multifaceted. A significant shift in the focus of a state's reform and improvement effort is usually the result of a confluence of indicators that all point to a common need. For example, the current focus on reading improvement in Illinois is not a unique trend in America. A few of the forces that guided the Illinois State Board of Education's decision to focus on reading are listed here:

• Data from the NAEP indicated that the nation's performance in reading was not improving.

• Data from the National Adult Literacy Survey (NALS) indicated that millions of adults in Illinois and in the nation were illiterate.

• Illinois Goal Assessment Program data indicated that reading achievement in Illinois was declining.

• National and state level efforts to set content and performance standards in reading and language arts were drawing attention to the wide range of instructional practices and expectations that existed between and among schools and districts in a single state. With this discovery came the growing awareness that differential learning opportunities and expectations created huge differences in performance. Lowest performing students tended to be concentrated in low-income urban and rural regions.

• State and national leaders in literacy and assessment agreed that higher expectations and opportunities, applied consistently, might lead to increases in literacy learning and achievement.

• Research results were beginning to point to a set of instructional practices that seemed to be effective in reducing the numbers of students in kindergarten through third grade who were identified as struggling or failing readers.

- Some states had already begun to raise their expectations and to work to systematically improve early reading instruction. Some of their early results were promising.

- At the federal level, the Governor's Summit on Education and the President's Goals 2000 initiative each highlighted reading as an area where improvement efforts would be focused.

- A panel of six national experts, brought together in the Illinois Reading Summit, agreed that literacy learning and achievement in America and in Illinois were unnecessarily low, that there was sufficient research to warrant research-based changes in reading instruction, and that improvements in instruction should be focused on students in kindergarten through third grade.

- When Illinois legislators visited local schools and talked with their constituents, they learned that the reading problems they had heard about were real, existed in their own communities, and deserved their support and attention.

Each of these individual forces came together to produce sufficient public pressure to warrant a shift in the state's educational priorities. This is just one example of the kind of converging evidence that is usually behind any new or changing focus in a state's efforts in improving or reforming education.

Does this suggest that states are stubborn, reluctant to change, or recalcitrant when it comes to agreeing to do things different or better? No! It means that states are cautious, and require compelling evidence from a variety of independent sources to agree to shift their attention or effort. Change is enacted with cautious confidence based on data, research, and converging evidence.

What You Can Do

Be informative and be informed! Read about and keep current with the trends in your field. Adopt a national perspective and monitor trends in literacy as well as in other areas that affect you. When state and national reports are released, read them and share them with your colleagues. Look for trends with your colleagues. Discuss how national reports, research findings, and assessment results are or are not reflected in your own communities. Share your observations with your colleagues, state department employees, and state legislators.

When a shift in your state's educational priorities is being considered, ask why. Review the evidence that is contributing to the decision-making process. Contribute to the conversation. If you are convinced or compelled by the evidence, if you believe that the shift in focus will be a good thing for your local community, speak up in support of the efforts for reform. Conversely, if you do not feel that there is sufficient evidence, or if you are not convinced that the evidence supports a major shift in a state's educational focus, you need to let your local policy makers know. Show them the data (or lack of data). Remember, you are the expert! If you do not think that the data are sufficiently compelling to warrant your changing your priorities, practices, and procedures, it is up to you to let your state education agency and your legislative representatives know. If you believe change is warranted, then contribute your own voice to help create public confidence in the new direction.

PROVIDING RESOURCES AND PROFESSIONAL DEVELOPMENT OPPORTUNITIES

Most state education agencies spend a great deal of time and money to provide professional development opportunities and to develop and distribute resources for educators, administrators, students, and families. Almost every state in the nation has adopted state level content and performance standards. In a well-planned system, all of the professional development programs, state-sponsored publications, events, and resources are aligned to the state's standards. Descriptions of programs and publications illustrate for educators how they are aligned to the state's standards and how they can be used to support local improvement efforts.

In Illinois, the Division of Reading has produced and distributed Reading Kits for classroom teachers in prekindergarten through third grade, bilingual or English as a Second Language (ESL) resource teachers, primary reading specialists, and elementary principals. Illinois educators, teacher educators, and curriculum specialists have designed the kits. Each kit includes

- one to three professional books,
- a classroom teaching resource,
- a collection of teaching strategies,
- a collection of research articles,
- a teaching demonstration videotape modeling the strategies described in the collection of strategies,
- two or three children's books that are referenced in the collection of teaching strategies,

- the Illinois Learning Standards for language arts, and
- one or two externally published monographs on literacy.

The kits are updated annually. Resources in the kits are featured as part of the state's statewide professional development programs for classroom teachers, administrators, and paraprofessionals. Any new publications or programs are analyzed with respect to three criteria:

1. Are they aligned to existing resources?

2. Do they make a unique contribution to the system?

3. Are they aligned to the Illinois Learning Standards?

If the candidate product does not meet all three criteria, it is not added to the system of professional development programs and resources. Excerpts from the kits and kit contents lists can be downloaded from the Illinois State Board of Education site <http://www.illinoisreads.org/>.

In California, the San Diego Office of Education has developed two online professional development series. The first is entitled Teaching Reading in Every Classroom (TREC). It is a series of 16 programs intended for fourth through eighth grade teachers of students who are reading below level. The series was developed in collaboration with TREC. Visit the TREC Web site <http://www.pdop.org/trec/> for more information.

The second series, Reading in Secondary Education (RISE), consists of nine programs. Classroom examples that are included in the series are taken from teachers and schools that have significantly improved reading achievement at their schools. Contact jslater@sdcoe.k12.ca.us for more information.

Staff development opportunities should be designed for specific audiences. One-size-fits-all staff development is not effective. In Maryland and Illinois, the state departments of education sponsor special principals' institutes on reading improvement. Several states have begun to provide professional development opportunities for their paraprofessional staff. In Texas and Illinois, professional development opportunities for teachers are ongoing and are offered through a network of regional service providers. Texas is providing ongoing inservice in reading for regional service providers to strengthen their capacity to deliver consistent, research-based professional development statewide. This model is one that has been adopted by several other states as well, including Ohio and Illinois. Visit your state's Web site to find out what professional development opportunities are available.

What You Can Do

Find out what resources are available. Find out how you can access the resources for yourself and for your colleagues. If you have the opportunity, attend state or regional conferences where state education agency staff are describing the state's literacy program, products, and resources. If you have trouble accessing your state's resources, or if you have trouble finding out about resources and opportunities, you need to notify your state education agency and request that additional resources be made available or that they be distributed differently or in different quantities. Ask to be added to mailing lists and e-mail lists. Monitor state Web sites. If your state has a regional intermediate delivery system, find out what resources and opportunities are available through these providers. Add your name and address to any mailing or distribution lists these organizations sponsor.

TEXTBOOK ADOPTION, TEXTBOOK LOAN PROGRAMS, AND SUPPORT FOR SCHOOL AND CLASSROOM LIBRARIES

State education agencies play a variety of roles in selecting and purchasing textbooks. In states that have textbook adoption programs, a list of endorsed textbooks is developed and schools choosing to purchase textbooks on the endorsed lists may use approved funding sources to purchase those texts. Schools electing to purchase textbooks not included on the adoption list must find other means to pay for those books.

In states that do not have adoption and endorsement programs, textbook selection is a local decision that is made at the district or building level. In many cases, these states run purchasing cycles that determine what years a district can purchase books for which subjects and which grades. This cyclical purchasing calendar is used to make sure that textbooks are kept as current as possible and that all subjects are updated on a timely basis. Funding equations for book purchases are based on enrollment figures.

Local, state, and federal funds are combined to help schools purchase textbooks and school and classroom library books. Decisions are made at the local level that determine what proportion of the local budget is spent on textbooks and library books. Funds from state, federal, and private grants can often be combined with state and federal funds to supplement the purchase of textbooks and library books.

In California, two groups review materials for inclusion on the materials adoption lists. The Instructional Materials Committee consists of approximately 108 members. The Content Review Panel includes 16 members. Training is provided for each group prior to the selection process. In addition, there are 24 Resource Display Center sites located throughout the state where materials that have been submitted for consideration can be reviewed.

California has also begun publishing a list of recommended literature. The Recommended Literature: Kindergarten Through Grade Twelve list includes more than 2,700 titles in six languages. The list is available on the California Department of Education Web site <http://www.cde.ca. gov/>.

What You Can Do

There are three things teachers can do to take an active role in the textbook procurement process in their school or district:

1. be informed,

2. participate, and

3. be aggressive.

Every teacher needs to know which texts are purchased when and what funding sources are available to fund purchases. Textbook purchasing schedules and funding sources are usually available from your principal or from the office in your district that coordinates textbook purchases. Find out when textbook review and selection committees begin their work and volunteer to work as a review committee member, to pilot programs or texts in your classroom, or to give feedback on your review of potential programs. Check to see if your state education agency or intermediate regional provider has any textbook selection tools or guidelines that can inform your work. If you teach in a state that has a system of learning standards, make sure that your decision is informed by how well the textbooks being reviewed are aligned to your state and local learning and performance standards.

There are grants available from the federal government, at the state level, through private foundations, and through professional organizations including the IRA, the ALA, and the NCTE. If your district has a staff person assigned to lead grant writing activities, work with that person to make sure that you and your colleagues are notified when there are grant opportunities that will fund the purchase of books for your school or district. If your district and school are not already active in competing for grant funds, meet with your principal to discuss how you can begin working to tap into this funding source. Persevere! There is a saying that money gets money. While your first few attempts may not be successful, once you begin to secure grant funding, it will become easier to secure additional grants. When you are applying, do not be afraid to ask the funding source for models of successful proposals from previous years that will inform your work.

CONVENING STATEWIDE MEETINGS, ADVISORY BOARDS, REVIEW COMMITTEES, AND TASK FORCES

Typically, there are one to five staff members at a state education agency who are assigned to work on reading. More often than not, reading is just one of their responsibilities. They might also work as Title I state coordinators, as Even Start coordinators, or as staff to the Comprehensive School Reform program. State education agencies rely a great deal on the advice and feedback they receive from their advisory boards, review committees, working committee focus groups, and task forces to assist them with their work.

In Ohio, as part of that state's reading initiative, Ohio Reads, five networks have been established to support the work of the initiative and the implementation of standards-based instruction in reading. A sixth network will soon be added. The five networks are professional development, literacy specialists, principal's literacy, curriculum alignment, and parent academies. The sixth network will be an early literacy network.

In Maryland, four networks focus on best practice and research-based professional development for those who teach primary, intermediate, secondary, and adult reading.

In Illinois, a task force of teacher educators, university administrators, legislators, classroom teachers, and reading specialists are preparing a report to the governor and state superintendent of education aligning teacher education in reading with Illinois's new standards-based certification requirements for classroom teachers and reading specialists.

In Texas, teams of business leaders, educators, parents, reading specialists, and researchers contributed to the design for a statewide reading initiative that was called for by former governor of Texas, President George W. Bush.

What You Can Do

Get involved! Each of the committees described here includes a number of teachers and reading specialists. There are many things you can do to secure an appointment to a state level committee. The most obvious way is to meet and get to know state education agency staff and to ask to be included in any upcoming committees, task forces, or focus groups. State level staff get quite a few of these requests, so it will help to provide examples of the kind of work you are doing at the local level and an idea of what you will contribute to the state's efforts. Follow up on your initial contact to let the state staff know that you would also welcome the opportunity to review any draft documents or programs for them.

You can also get involved through your state level legislators. Meet with one of your local legislators, give them your résumé and a few ideas about what to include in a letter of nomination, and ask them to write a letter nominating you to serve as a committee member. You might also ask your principal, superintendent, or regional intermediate provider staff member to nominate you to serve as a committee member.

Keep in mind that committees are small and that you may have to wait a while before you hear anything. If you know anyone who already serves on a state level committee, ask them to pass on your name and to reinforce your commitment to become involved.

CREATING AND SUSTAINING PARTNERSHIPS THAT SUPPORT TEACHING AND LEARNING

Partnerships are essential to statewide improvement initiatives. They let the state agency capitalize on existing networks and channels of communication. They guarantee the support of important leaders. They ensure that multiple perspectives and issues are addressed by statewide initiatives. They ensure that state level initiatives reflect the cultural, economic, and linguistic diversity of the state. They allow the agency to work as efficiently as possible. And they guarantee much greater levels of visibility, awareness, and acceptance of new initiatives than a state agency would typically generate on its own. Broad-based ownership of a state's education efforts is critical to the success of the agency's work. State education agencies depend on strategic partnerships including but not limited to state level professional organizations (e.g., National Education Association [NEA] & Illinois Federation of Teachers [IFT] affiliates & state level affiliates of the IRA, the NCTE, & the NAEYC):

- teacher-educator associations,
- state organizations of school administrators,
- state level special educators' associations,
- state level bilingual and ESL organizations,
- state level PTAs,
- state level adult and family literacy organizations,

- state level library associations,
- state networks of intermediate service providers,
- privately funded literacy related organizations, and
- community-based organizations that provide before- and after-school care.

In addition to partnerships with all of these education related organizations, successful state agencies also forge strong partnerships with the office of the governor, the state legislature, state level business roundtables, state and local real estate groups, and business and community service organizations.

In Ohio, as part of Governor Bob Taft's education initiative, Ohio Reads, a call went out for more than 20,000 volunteers to provide one-on-one tutoring in Ohio's schools. Currently, more than 27,000 trained volunteer reading tutors are hard at work in local tutoring programs. Most volunteers tutor a child once a week for 30 to 60 minutes. Tutoring takes place before, during, and after school, as well as on weekends and in the evenings. Scheduling is designed by individual schools and communities to meet their local needs.

What You Can Do

Work to facilitate awareness and involvement. Make sure that organizations that reflect your community's perspectives, culture, and values are included in state partnerships. Solicit and encourage these partnerships. Share publications, resources, and news of the state's efforts with your local organizations. If you have reviewed the available resources and opportunities and suspect that your state's efforts do not reflect the needs of a particular organization, work with representatives of the organization to make their needs known to the state agency. Partnerships really do enhance the effectiveness of your state education agency.

LITERACY IS THE CORNERSTONE OF DEMOCRACY

There are a number of opportunities for you to become an active partner in your state education agency's reading improvement efforts. The success of these efforts will be enhanced and expanded by increased participation from the state's educators.

In a democracy, literacy really is everyone's business. Whether or not our children learn to read and choose to read throughout their lives should matter to each and every person in our communities. We need the support of all of our community members to support our children's improving literacy. As educators, it is our responsibility to stimulate the interest and awareness of our legislators, parents, and community members in supporting our efforts to improve our communities' and states' literacy teaching and learning. We are working to see that all of our children learn to read.

To Reflect

1. How do the ideas presented in Chapter 6 relate to your teaching experiences?

2. What ideas support and confirm what you are already doing?

3. What did you find in this chapter that you can share with colleagues?

4. Did something suggest new possibilities for your program?

5. What questions does this chapter raise for further discussion and reflection?

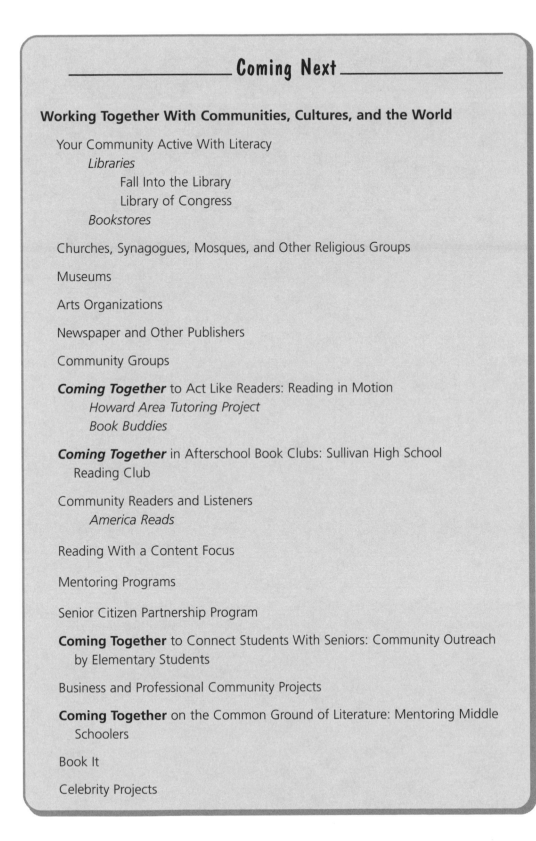

_____ **Coming Next** _____

Working Together With Communities, Cultures, and the World

Your Community Active With Literacy
    Libraries
        Fall Into the Library
        Library of Congress
    Bookstores

Churches, Synagogues, Mosques, and Other Religious Groups

Museums

Arts Organizations

Newspaper and Other Publishers

Community Groups

Coming Together to Act Like Readers: Reading in Motion
    Howard Area Tutoring Project
    Book Buddies

Coming Together in Afterschool Book Clubs: Sullivan High School
    Reading Club

Community Readers and Listeners
    America Reads

Reading With a Content Focus

Mentoring Programs

Senior Citizen Partnership Program

Coming Together to Connect Students With Seniors: Community Outreach
    by Elementary Students

Business and Professional Community Projects

Coming Together on the Common Ground of Literature: Mentoring Middle
    Schoolers

Book It

Celebrity Projects

Learning From and With One Another

Cyberage Connections

Continuing to Look Outward

To Reflect

● ● ●

Working Together With Communities, Cultures, and the World

YOUR COMMUNITY ACTIVE WITH LITERACY

The nature and meaning of what we mean by community continues to evolve. No longer defined as the people within the immediate confines of our locality, the word community has come to mean people we can connect with, people we affect, and people who affect us. With the possibilities travel and instant communication afford us, we feel closer to and part of the world and many cultures. In our own communities and schools, we can learn with and from people with different backgrounds. The community is the context that can help students understand and appreciate the importance of literacy. Think about what literacy resources are near your school (see Figure 7.1). Many opportunities exist for the school to connect with the community outside the school's walls and around the world.

Encourage your students to visit places listed in Figure 7.1 and report back to the class about moments of literacy they observed. Consider keeping a list in your classroom of places you and your students have visited. If possible, take class field trips to local newspaper publishers, bookstores, and libraries.

Places to Come Together
as Readers

- Public library

- Local newspaper

- Bookstores

- Businesses with signs and regular employee uses of reading

- Music shops

- Restaurants and coffee bars with reading nooks

- Stores that feature and sell Oprah's Book Club selections

- Stores that sell children's books

- Churches, mosques, synagogues, and other places to practice religion

- Internet cafés

- Post offices and mail stations

- Museums

What can you add from your community?

_____

_____

_____

_____

Figure 7.1

Libraries

As you begin a new school year with students, it is a good idea to make a connection with the public library. The public library is an important resource for the school.

- The public library has a lot of good books and other resources that often go well beyond what the individual school library can contain.

- The public library is often part of a larger city or area network and can access books on specific topics for individual and class use.

- The public library has many technological resources—families can access the Internet and get CD-ROMs and videos for home use.

Fall Into the Library

Each fall in some communities, elementary classes visit the library. Parents and children are encouraged to get library cards. Sending home information about the opportunities at the local library can help nudge parents to take advantage of this resource.

Throughout the school year, there are programs and special guests at many libraries that are of interest to the school. Staying connected with the library means having greater resources. Libraries often highlight new books and provide lists of good books for different ages and different interests. The resources of the library can save teachers much time and effort.

Library of Congress

The U.S. Library of Congress offers extensive services, information, and special programs that will increase students' interest in reading. For example, in September 2001, the Library of Congress and First Lady Laura Bush hosted the first National Book Festival, an event where reading was celebrated and encouraged. Now an annual event, the festival features authors in all genres of children's and adult books, and tapes of many of the sessions are available on the Web site. The first lady is also Honorary Chair of a national reading promotion campaign. In effect through 2003, the theme Telling America's Stories is promoted through the Center for the Book, which promotes reading and literacy through affiliated centers throughout the nation (see <http://www.loc.gov/loc/cfbook/> for more information). The Library of Congress currently features Poetry 180, an effort that asks America's high school students to devote time to reading aloud one poem a day (more information is available at <http://www. loc.gov/poetry/180/). For younger students, America's Story from America's Library is an interactive Web site filled with games,

puzzles, and rich histories of America (<http://www.americaslibrary.gov/cgi-bin/page.cgi>). For more on what the Library of Congress can offer to your students, go to the main Web site at <http://www.loc.gov.>.

Bookstores

It is energizing as adults to attend sessions and book signings by authors; we can take our stories and experiences back to school and share them with students to stimulate their vision of adult interest in authors and books. We can also attend sessions by authors who write both for adults and children. Larger bookstores often bring children's authors for talks and book signings. Some of these bookstores will network with schools so authors who come into the area can also visit schools.

Local bookstores also provide space to hold our reading council meetings. What a nice opportunity to combine a relaxed evening in the midst of books while we discuss literacy issues. Informed booksellers can be great resources themselves. They know what books are coming out, which are best for particular interests, and what other resources link with books. Some bookstores even have children's literature specialists who can guide teachers in finding just the right books and resources needed for special projects. Some will even visit schools and attend professional meetings to speak with teachers.

CHURCHES, SYNAGOGUES, MOSQUES, AND OTHER RELIGIOUS GROUPS

The Torah, Koran, and Bible are central to the study and practice of Judaism, Islam, and Christianity, respectively. Children can learn a great deal about the value of literacy and the importance of literacy in the preservation of religious wisdom and history. By examining the different holy texts, students can also see how writing serves and follows different conventions—different orthographies, different organization on the page (right to left or left to right), and different markings for vowels and relationships of words. At the most basic level, however, young children can gain an appreciation for how these texts help maintain the faith and tradition of the believers. Literacy is central to these world religions.

MUSEUMS

I have had the great fortune of working with the Art Institute of Chicago on special projects linking reading and the arts. The children's services division worked with us on an integrated curriculum project over a two-year period where we helped children develop the following abilities:

- use inquiry skills when viewing works of art,
- think across works of art to link them together thematically,
- find thematic connections among different pieces, and
- express their responses to viewing art in writing.

We attended seminars presented by museum staff, worked with them in creating activities for students, and used artifacts they had in their loan program to take to the schools. We also engaged in a hands-on exhibit for children that explored key works of art from a variety of cultures. Instead of displaying hands-off collections of untouchable and unapproachable "jewels," museums are now trying to connect the public more actively with art and history. The Art Institute of Chicago offers teachers involved in their programs free passes. Other museums have similar programs. It is worthwhile to check how your local museums provide support for teachers and schoolwork.

Another way to enhance literacy is to take students on a "communications" tour of a local museum to study how the museum staff has provided written support to help viewers understand and appreciate the collection. Museums often engage the viewer by asking questions and creating an interactive environment for learning. For example, at the Museum of Natural History in New York City, the signs posted in the new dinosaur exhibit ask viewers as they enter a hall what they know about how dinosaurs walked, ate, and lived. While visiting the hall, viewers will encounter exhibits that will help viewers answer questions posed earlier. For example, comparing several fossilized dinosaur jaws can help viewers guess what dinosaurs ate.

Talking with students about how information is communicated takes their visits to a new level and focuses on content and literacy at the same time. As an extension, students can create their own guides to exhibits.

ARTS ORGANIZATIONS

Many cities have arts organizations that are also turning attention to literacy. In Chicago, Reading in Motion, a nonprofit educational organization dedicated to combining music, drama, and dance, has turned its attention to reading. Since 1997, Reading in Motion, formerly Whirlwind, has been working with schools to find ways to combine the arts with language arts. See Coming Together to Act Like Readers.

NEWSPAPERS AND OTHER PUBLISHERS

Visits to local publishers help students appreciate the complexity of publishing the materials that we read daily. Many local papers are eager to teach students about their community resources. Nearly every newspaper offers an opportunity for students to see in a very concrete way the process of publishing. This can provide the motivation for children to create their own classroom newspapers.

In newspapers, there are often stories in special sections written at an easy enough level to make them valuable resources for classroom projects and studies. Check your local paper to see if there are ways you can introduce students to a community literacy resource they may not know about.

Visits to the school by news writers and editors can also be informative. For example, a sportswriter from one of the national syndicated press services explained his work and the pressures on writers to a class. The students, and particularly the sports enthusiasts among them, were fascinated by learning what a sportswriter's work entails. It also opened their eyes to an expanded possibility of jobs for the future and how literacy takes many forms.

COMMUNITY GROUPS

Many community groups are interested in literacy and in supporting students who find reading difficult. Such groups may provide a valuable support for ongoing public school literacy programs. Boys and Girls Clubs, community tutoring programs through churches and service clubs, and extended school projects funded through the U.S. government's 21st Century Community Learning Centers Program are all potential supports for literacy.

Coming Together to Act Like Readers

Reading in Motion

—Karl Androes

Reading in Motion was originally named Whirlwind Performance Company and founded as a nonprofit arts organization in January 1983 by three artists. In November of 2003 Whirlwind officially changed its name to Reading in Motion, which more closely reflects the organization's current mission of teaching reading through the arts.

From the earliest days, the organization's founders, who include current Executive Director Karl Androes, created programming for students based on the belief that children can learn basic skills through the arts

In the mid-90s it became clear to Androes and the board of directors that the biggest challenge facing students was their poor reading skills. After much study and research, the company began to shift its educational focus toward improving the reading skills of children, especially those in the Chicago Public Schools. Reading in Motion continued to develop its acclaimed arts-based reading curricula over the next several years and in 1997 we widened our scope to include the training of teachers in order to reach an even larger number of students. Reading in Motion currently offers both afterschool and summer workshops for teachers wishing to learn how to implement our curricula in their own classrooms.

Reading research shows that reaching children early in life has been proven to be the most effective way to positively impact their development. Therefore, 2003 saw the company refocus its educational efforts more closely on the critical kindergarten through third grade years. Using the best current reading research and our 20 years of experience in teaching children to read through dance, drama, and music, we began developing a new, more comprehensive reading program for the primary grades. The new program, called Benchmarks, envisions students beginning our curriculum in kindergarten and continuing with it through the third grade. The goal for this program is to have students reading at or above grade level at the end of each and every year.

Benchmarks

In development since 2003, Benchmarks is Reading in Motion's newest response to the urgent need for effective reading intervention. Designed as a four-year supplemental reading curriculum following students from kindergarten through third grade, its specific goal is to bring 100% of students to grade level by the end of third grade. Reading in Motion instructors train classroom teachers to implement the curriculum, allowing them to transform the reading performance of the school as a whole.

Like its predecessors at Reading in Motion, Benchmarks is arts based: its carefully crafted music- and drama-based activities inspire children to actively participate in reading exercises while also teaching them self-control and teamwork. Student work is split between whole group activities, independent work areas, and intensive small group work to address each child's specific instructional needs. In addition, family members are also trained to support their children through a series of Family Literacy Workshops.

Howard Area Tutoring Project

As an example, the Howard Area Tutoring Project, begun by Darrell Morris, is located in a low-income area in north Chicago. Darrell began the project as a new faculty member at National-Louis University. He was committed to enhancing literacy opportunities for children from less-affluent communities and finding ways to help all children become readers. To this end, he developed the tutoring project linked to the Chicago Public Schools in a very low-income neighborhood. He decided to focus the reading support on second grade students so they would have support in early literacy development. With the help of a selfless volunteer director, Bev Shaw, and a dedicated set of volunteer tutors the project has continued now for over 20 years. The project works collaboratively with the neighborhood school. Each fall, all the second graders coming into the school are diagnosed for reading development. Children with the lowest literacy skills are selected and matched with tutors for individual work twice a week after school. The tutors are all volunteers from the area, many of whom have teaching degrees and some with advanced work in reading. (The project also supports the reading program at National-Louis University by giving university students an opportunity to work with urban children and become involved in a city school.) Lessons for the twice weekly sessions are developed by the reading specialists who coordinate the project based on feedback from the sessions. Tutors conduct the sessions and keep records of the students' progress. A full description of this powerful support model is available in the *Howard Street Tutoring Manual* (Morris, 2005).

Book Buddies

Another project that uses volunteer community tutors to assist beginning readers is the University of Virginia Book Buddies program. In this project, adult tutors are trained to provide specific beginning reading support and engage students in word study and a variety of reading skill development activities. Having university students work with young readers makes some strong connections that are personal and motivating. Tutors report learning more about literacy themselves and appreciate the project opportunities to contribute to the community. Book Buddies (Johnson, Invernezzi, & Juel, 1998) gives clear explanations for tutors.

The Howard Area Tutoring Project and the Virginia Book Buddies program represent how reading educators have been able to develop strong tutoring programs so concerned community members can contribute to literacy in important ways. There are many programs throughout the country that involve tutors and community members working with students to support their literacy. Some of these programs take place in the school, and many occur beyond the school day in community locations. Think about your own school needs; it may be that you can link productively with some community group and provide a rich added resource for your students. At the least, you may be able to compile a list of students who would benefit from tutoring. Working with community groups can be a valuable outreach of the school's energy too. Often volunteers are very eager to make their programs as rich and valuable as possible to the children they tutor.

Coming Together in Afterschool Book Clubs

Sullivan High School Reading Club

—Suzanne Zweig

In every one of the 75 Chicago public high schools, once a year a famous alum or well-known person serves as principal for a day. About five years ago, Mayor Richard M. Daley was principal for a day at Orr High School. As principal, the mayor was asked to participate in the school's book club. He so loved the program that he decided that all Chicago high schools should have the chance to have a book club.

Consequently, the Department of Libraries at Chicago Public Schools developed a grant program, which offers $1,000 in matching funds for schools to start chapters of Mayor Daley's Book Club, an afterschool reading club for teens.

At Sullivan High School we were able to get the matching funds, which allowed for our book club to get underway. The first year was incredibly successful. Twelve kids took part in the afterschool sessions with me and another teacher, John Butler. It was terrific! We read the hottest new adolescent fiction, including the following books:

- *Monster,*
- *Twelve Shots,*
- *Blood and Chocolate,*
- *The Story of Miss Jane Pittman,* and
- *Killer Cousin.*

The discussions were wonderful. The kids were so honest and forthcoming. Part of the money for the club was used to give the participants T-shirts with the book cover emblazoned on them.

The following year, there wasn't any money available directly from CPS [Chicago Public Schools], but Mayor Daley recruited many sponsors who helped pay for books. The titles of the books the second year were chosen by the board and sent to us each month. These books were less compelling to the kids than the ones we had chosen. So, with the help of our principal Kathy Ruffalo, we received money every month to purchase books, which included the following:

- *Kindred,*
- *The Color of Water,*
- *A Lesson Before Dying,*
- *Currents-Book of Poetry,* and
- *Who Killed Mr. Chippendale.*

The Sullivan High School Afterschool Book Club is alive and thriving. The club gives many kids the opportunity to discuss good books—a "privilege" that was previously hard to come by. Interestingly, everyone who participated spoke. At the end of the year, kids made suggestions about which books to discuss the following year. Some kids went on to explore other titles by authors we read.

The most important aspect of the afterschool reading club was the connections the kids made and the pleasure they took in talking about a good book. I truly believe that we were all enriched by the experience of participating in the book club.

COMMUNITY READERS AND LISTENERS

There have been wonderful projects bringing adults in to the schools as readers and book buddies for years. Community leaders reading in classrooms highlights the reality that significant adults value reading and do it regularly. Some schools regularly bring in members of the community: a fireman, a local religious leader, the mayor, a city council member, athletes, and leaders of civic groups. (See Coming Together in Afterschool Book Clubs.) The principal coming into classrooms and sharing his or her favorite book reinforces that adults are readers.

More recently, a focus on having adults come to the schools to read individually with children has extended this idea much more personally. It has also added the value of community members establishing personal relations with children around literacy. One retirement home in our community has had a long-standing relationship with the local school. Each week, seniors come to the school to read with their buddies. Prior to each visit, the teacher helps students pick out books that can be read with the help of the adult. Some teachers assign buddies to readers who are not confident and need practice. Other teachers identify students who need more personal adult attention and use the partnering as a way of supplementing the rich exchanges students need. Another area senior citizen center invites a classroom of children to come to their center and read to the seniors. These monthly visits are also powerful ways community members make long and meaningful connections around literacy.

America Reads

The America Reads Program of the federal government has stimulated a great deal of interest in bringing students and other community members into schools as reading partners. Under this program, college students can get work credit to help repay student loans by working in schools. Other funded America Reads projects do not have a good pool of students and so enlist other community members to be readers and listeners. In whatever way the programs operate—in school or beyond—these projects have stimulated a great deal of adult engagement in the literacy lives of children.

READING WITH A CONTENT FOCUS

As children move into the intermediate grades, the need for good reading intensifies. Textbooks with different organization and structure, dense content, and specific vocabulary are added to the more predictable fiction in a student's reading. Teachers find that not only is the content of the material new, but the different structures make reading more threatening to less-than-confident students. Using adults to support students' informational reading is a natural extension of the reading buddies idea.

One project in New York, the After School Reading Partners Program, was designed for fourth grade students needing a bridge to successful content reading and learning. Since social studies seemed to be a particular need, Lynn Gelzheiser and Christopher d'Angelo, State University of New York at Albany, developed a program to support readers at this level. To help students become better readers and learn more about New York state history, they developed units that tutors and children could enjoy together. The hope was that the adult tutor would also be a link to real history of the state; these adults could speak about the history from a more personal perspective and help the children make connections. They organized the materials the tutors and children would use in an interesting manner to help the students gain confidence in reading history. They collected three kinds of books to be read for each unit: one storybook or picture book that presented one or two social studies concepts or vocabulary terms, one informational book, and one pleasure reading novel on the theme (Gelzheiser & d'Angelo, 2000).

The tutors are instructed in how to relate to their students and how to encourage their acquisition of both content and reading strategies in an initial learning session. In addition, they receive a guide that can help them adjust their coaching to the students' increasing independence during the year. The units all follow a similar format. Students begin by reading the easy storybook or books. Then they read the nonfiction trade book. The last reading is from the novel or biography that relates to the theme. The project tries to have more than one text of each type so students can make some personal selection of materials to read.

This model seems so sensible and strong. Students need a great deal of help moving into content learning; tutors using a well-structured program can provide tremendous support in this process and can make the learning of content personally interesting and engaging.

MENTORING PROGRAMS

Many schools now have mentoring programs to help build stronger supportive relationships for students with adults who show care for their development. When these projects also use reading and writing as a major component, they can be significant in helping children value literacy. (See Coming Together on the Common Ground of Literature.)

SENIOR CITIZEN PARTNERSHIP PROGRAM

Seniors can be of great help to children, and children in turn offer a great deal to seniors. Karen Mead, a fourth grade teacher in Stanton, Iowa, has developed a project that provides rich reciprocal rewards to both groups. Her daughter planted the seeds of the idea in her head when she was working in the kitchen of the Care Center as a high school student. "You should get to know them and take your students there," her daughter admonished.

Coming Together to Connect Students With Seniors

Community Outreach by Elementary Students

—Karen Mead

I teach fourth grade in Stanton, Iowa, a small community with a rich Swedish tradition. The "adopted grandparents" project I have developed as an authentic context for reading and language arts was suggested by my daughter. As a high school student, she worked part time in the kitchen of the local nursing home, the Stanton Care Center. My daughter would come back from work and tell her me about the interesting people she was meeting. She felt that the people were "so neat" that she strongly nudged me to bring my fourth graders to the center to "adopt" them. (This daughter now teaches autistic children in West Des Moines, Iowa.)

Initially, I was quite nervous about working with the elderly. It didn't take long, however, before I saw the joy of the relationships and the possibilities the project held. I have continued to refine and develop the program over the last 14 years. Every other Friday afternoon my fourth grade class walks to the Care Center, which is just a few blocks from the school, and engages in a variety of activities with their "adopted grandparents." These activities stimulate the children's abilities to communicate in a variety of ways with elderly people and help me make our reading and language arts goals meaningful to them.

Making a Lasting Match

Because I have been working in the Center for so long now, I know the residents quite well. And after two to three weeks with a new class, I also know my students well enough to match them with the seniors. Bonnie Newton, the Center's activities director, also helps select the partners. Appropriate pairings are important because the adopted grandparents' relationships will last an entire school year.

Getting to Know You

To help the students and the Center's residents get acquainted, students conduct a structured interview that I have developed. Interviewing residents helps students see that their older partners have lead rich lives. Before coming to interview the adults, I talk with the students about how to conduct the interviews and take notes. After interviewing their senior partners, the students write a biographical sketch of their special resident.

The students introduce themselves to the seniors by creating a booklet, which is really their own autobiographical sketch, called "Who Am I." The students give the booklet as a gift to the resident they adopt. I found that when students include pictures of themselves in the booklet the seniors are more able remember the students and make connections with them.

Making Curriculum Connections

Sharing books is another way to make connections early in the year. We begin by having the students select picture books and other highly illustrated books to read with their seniors. The books give them something in common to talk about. The students learn that picture books aren't just for children who are very young. Many picture books are very meaningful and thought provoking. Students begin to think more about the purposes for reading and what makes good sharing. In the process they become more careful in their own book selection. Later in the year, the partners read or recite poetry to each other. (See Schedule of Activities With Adopted Grandparents.) This is important to me because I want to pass my love of poetry to my students. I love coming around to the residents' rooms as children and seniors share these literacy experiences. The neatest thing is that the grandparents brag about the readers to me as I roam the Center checking on the activity. The children gain such status from being praised!

Reading and sharing books is important for the children. So, too, are the writing and oral language skills they develop. Learning to introduce themselves to adults, developing skills in conversation, giving directions for joint projects, and performing for the seniors are important aspects of language arts. I find that this partnership also provides a real audience for children's writing. They interview and create biographical sketches, write their own autobiographies, and develop messages for holidays and special events. The real purpose for writing is all imbedded in the project activities.

As the project has evolved, I have developed a set of activities for each month, which vary by the year and our current interests. Some are craft projects the partners can do together, such as making Halloween jack-o'-lanterns and baking cookies. Others involve reflection on life in the early twentieth century and contrasting that to children's lives today. Some involve sharing talents and celebrating special events.

I have learned that all these activities help students learn to communicate with older people. The children are always kind and build touching relationships with their "grandparents." For example, when the class was busy making a math symmetry project, the students asked, "Mrs. Mead, can't we make one for our grandparents, too?" Later, when conducting a plant sale, they asked to bring some plants to the Care Center to share. These relationships have become an important part of the students' lives, not to mention the positive effect they have had on the "grandparents." The whole project has also provided a generative center for my efforts to make reading and language arts meaningful to my students.

Schedule of Activities With Adopted Grandparents

September

- Orientation to care center: Interview the new "grandparents" and share favorite books with residents.

October

- Fall leaf project: sponge painting. This keeps all actively engaged and working together. The students learn how to do the painting before they go to the center and then they teach the residents.
- Pumpkin project: seniors and students decorate pumpkins together. Community members and groups donate the pumpkins. The students learn how to decorate and then do it with their seniors.

November

- Read books together. Teacher guides students to select books that will promote discussion and contain content that is interesting.
- Thanksgiving. Kids memorize poems and do choral reading.

December

- Cookies. Cookies are made prior to going to visiting the center, then decorated with seniors, and eaten together in a real celebration.

January

- Historical reflection: What life was like when the seniors were growing up. Discussion is centered on how the world changed over the course of the twentieth century. There is no better way to gain perspective on history than to interview seniors who have lived it. After their interviews with the seniors the students come back and share what they learned with the class.

- Partners create bird feeders together.

February

- Valentine's Day: Students help residents make Valentines they want to give to others.
- Toys: The students share their own toys with their partners. Kids have to explain how their toy works and what it does. They prepare and learn to do the explanation. (Residents are fascinated with the remote control and computer games.)

March

- Reading Poetry Together: Students find some poems they like and read with seniors. Seniors often know many poems and can share their memories of favorites with the students.
- Plant seeds.
- St. Patrick's Party.
- Talent Show: Students prepare their own talent "acts." Residents share their own talents if they wish.

April

- Easter: Students and seniors dye eggs together.

May

- Lunch during National Nursing Home Week: the Center hosts a special lunch in the students' honor. Students sit with their "grandparents" and share the joy of the year's relationship.
- Rock painting: The partners paint rocks then put them in the outdoor courtyard so they can be enjoyed for the summer.

BUSINESS AND PROFESSIONAL COMMUNITY PROJECTS

The opportunities to connect with the larger business and professional community keep expanding. These groups seem to recognize how important involvement in education is to our future. A few years ago, Secretary of Education Richard Riley spearheaded efforts to connect schools with the larger communities (U.S. Department of Education Community Update). All community groups were encouraged to participate in sharing talents, time, and experiences to help strengthen local schools. As part of the annual America Goes Back to School initiative, one community asked the local chamber of commerce and the newspaper to lead an effort to encourage employers to give employees time off to take their children back to school and participate in the opening events of the school year.

Coming Together on the Common Ground of Literature

Mentoring Middle Schoolers

—Scott Waller, Curriculum Consultant and former Middle School Principal

Middle school students often benefit academically and personally from having mentors. However, mentoring relationships must be entered into carefully. We have learned a great deal from positive and less successful mentoring experiences.

Most mentoring programs put two people together who did not previously know each other. The success or failure of the program depends upon these two individuals finding a common interest around which they can build a relationship. [Taking] Participating in a mutually enjoyable activity (a ball game, theater, etc.) is a means for finding common ground for dialogue.

Literature provides another way to find this common ground. Most middle school students who have been recommended for a mentoring program have a difficult time opening up to adults because they commonly have had few good adult role models in their lives. Discussing a book, short story, or novel creates the framework for individuals to share and learn about each other's opinions and personal beliefs. Stories ranging from "Goldilocks and the Three Bears" to the Harry Potter books can promote discussions on any number of topics.

In addition, many students in mentoring programs are deficient readers. Using literature as a basis for discussion also promotes reading in a nonthreatening manner. The mentor and mentee can read the story together and discuss it. Some independent reading can follow up this shared reading between meetings. The curiosity piqued during the sessions often prompts the student to want to read on his or her own.

Structuring discussion about the readings is as important as the readings themselves. Adults tend to lead discussions in the direction they want them to go, which often serves to lessen mentee interest and input. A structure that invites the young person to lead the discussion and focuses on his or her insights and ideas will lead to a stronger mentor and mentee relationship. In addition, the use of reading strategies, such as Sketch to Stretch and Story Mapping, can help both parties make the most of the session's reading. It is important that both mentor and mentee undertake training before embarking on a mentoring relationship.

No mentoring program guarantees a match between the people involved no matter how well prepared or dedicated the individuals are. In mentoring, much like in friendship, there must be a match between the individuals involved. And just because a match doesn't fit, it does not mean the individuals are not suited for a mentoring program. If a match doesn't work, the two unsuited participants should be matched to another partner and try again.

The key to creating a good mentoring program is finding a good match between individuals and in creating a way for the individuals to communicate and get to know each other. From our experience with urban students, the care taken to create well defined programs leads to productive learning and deep relationships between the adults and students. The differences in student achievement and involvement in school like when they have mentors is clear.

- In rural Argentina there are few books available for children and no public libraries. Teachers developed "backpack libraries," collections of paperback books and magazines that they take from village to village. The teacher finds a place to display the books and magazines for the villagers to see and explore. Then children and adults can check out the books. After having them for a week or two in the village, the children and adults return the books to the "library." The teacher gets the backpack transported to the next village and the same process continues.

- In Beijing the English language teachers at Capitol Normal University are using adolescent novels to develop middle grade students' English abilities. With support from the New York State Reading Association, they now have a good collection of North American novels and have been able to translate some of them into Mandarin so the books are shown in both languages for the developing English learners. One adolescent told me that she loved reading the novels because "they gave me words to describe my feelings and confusions."

- In rural Tanzania I spent a summer helping secondary students prepare for the entrance exam that determined possible university admission. All high school courses and tests were in English even though that is at least the third language the students speak. I worked hard to help them review history, literature and writing, and science. I spent time working to develop their metacognitive sense of control over their study and test taking. The students had great fear of this test, and rightly so.

- In Russia my husband and I spent four years with excellent teachers who are trying to transform their traditional practices of giving lectures and become more student centered and constructivist in their classes. This Reading and Writing for Critical Thinking (RWCT) Project was sponsored by the International Reading Association (IRA) and funded by the Soros Foundation's Open Society Institute. The Russian teachers expressed the same tensions that U.S. teachers do regarding the need to cover a large amount of information and the need for students to become active learners.

- In Pakistan I worked on an educational project designed to create a new educational structure for Afghanistan after the Russians were defeated in 1989. Even at that time women were excluded from most education in rural and conservative areas on the Afghan-Pakistani border. The U.S. AID project required a component for women. That posed a real challenge, so "home schools" were established. Women teachers went into the walled compounds of extended families and established portable classrooms in corners of these homes. The teachers carried a small chalkboard, small writing pads, and charts with the alphabet silk-screened on large sheets of Pakistani cotton. A globe of heavy cotton and small books made of cotton were added resources for the teachers. I will always remember the eagerness of grandmothers, mothers, sisters, and young girls as they learned the alphabet and began to read.

The national organization Communities in Schools (CIS) is one example of how businesses are actively looking for ways to be of service to public schools. Its stated mission is "to champion the connection of needed community resources with schools to help young people successfully learn, stay in school, and prepare for life." Now in more than 150 cities and communities, each local organization creates a network of area businesses and organizations that are willing to be of service to the public schools. A survey of the CIS network showed that the majority of the projects across the nation are engaged with literacy and reading. A wide variety of projects develop in response to needs expressed by the schools for help from outside services to address obstacles faced by students and families.

One Chicago Big Brothers Big Sisters (BBBS) project reports the impact of connecting at-risk youth with positive role models. More than 85% of the partner schools in the Chicago projects have requested tutors or mentors for students. BBBS links high school students with elementary children and provides fun and educational support after school. The high school students tutor the elementary children and then join for monthly outings. The program also partners women professionals

International Educational Exchanges

The Fulbright Foundation sponsors an exchange program for teachers. Teachers apply and then spend a full year teaching in another country. Teachers from abroad come to the United States, and American teachers go abroad to teach in their schools.

The Japanese government sponsors two programs in honor of Fulbright through the Fulbright Memorial Foundation. Twice each year 50 teachers from across the United States are selected to visit schools in Japan and live in Japanese homes. One program is for three weeks and the other six.

The European Committee of the IRA has established a project so teachers can exchange with others in Europe. North American teachers wishing to also get ideas for possible contacts and exchanges will find this group helpful.

The Colorado Council of IRA sponsors annual exchanges for teachers from other countries to come to the United States and also helps U.S. teachers go abroad.

The Long Island Reading Council has established a partnership with Guatemalan teachers, helped them form the Guatemalan Reading Association, and now sends groups of teachers to Guatemala City two to three times a year to do workshops and help their associates in Guatemala. All teachers fund their own travel since the economy of Guatemala is very weak. In addition, since there are so few books or even pencils and paper in many schools in Guatemala, the council has earned money for classroom libraries and supplies by selling Guatemalan handicrafts at reading meetings and other events in the United States. They have been able to purchase more than 200 classroom libraries (books in Spanish) for schools desperately in need of resources through this ongoing effort.

---

with teenage girls at one school. These examples from CIS illustrate the potential when groups offer to partner with schools. (The national CIS office can be reached at 1-800-CIS-4Kids or on the Web at <http://www.cisnet.org/>.)

BOOK IT

This reading incentive program sponsored by Pizza Hut is an example of how businesses have found creative ways to encourage reading. While teachers and parents need to be aware that this brings a commercial product into the schools, it has been very effective in many schools in focusing students on reading more.

CELEBRITY PROJECTS

Reading is an interest to many Americans, including some of our celebrities. We are fortunate to have people like Dolly Parton and Tiger Woods support literacy efforts. Dolly Parton's Dollywood Foundation gives a book to each child born in her county in Tennessee each month during the first four years of their lives. They get the books, a special bookcase to house them, and encouragement to the parents to read with their children.

The Tiger Woods Foundation helps children believe in themselves through his program Start Something, which encourages children to realize and fulfill their dreams. Participants in the program complete five levels of character-building activities that include a promise to read for 20 minutes a day. Those who advance to the top level and show leadership abilities qualify to apply for a $10,000 scholarship and a variety of other incentives.

Jackie Joyner-Kersee is also supporting young children through her Boys and Girls Club in East St. Louis. It is designed with a gymnasium, wellness and fitness centers, a computer lab, and a library. Joyner-Kersee was inspired to create this center for young people by the pleasant association she had with the Mary Brown Center as a child. While she attended that center, she came in contact with people who helped her develop and who instilled her with values and morals. Now she is providing this same possibility for other children. Her example makes clear how important it

Electronic Exchanges

The world seems much smaller when we can use rapid technological communications to share with students and teachers in other parts of the globe. Many guidelines and cautions are provided in Burniske's (2000) book *Literacy in the Cyberage*. He suggests three basic purposes for telecollaborative learning:

1. interpersonal exchanges,

2. information collection, and

3. analysis and problem-solving projects.

Some informal exchanges have been started across continents by members of IRA who have linked informally with teachers in other parts of the world. The International Development Coordinating Committee for North America has prepared a guide with the names of teachers interested in such exchanges available at Btownsend@reading .org. Exchanges can open exciting new ideas and raise lots of questions for students to discuss. The book discussions often lead to even deeper exchanges among students as they face the reasons for their different points of view.

is for children to find in their community the literacy resources and the support they need to develop fully.

LEARNING FROM AND WITH ONE ANOTHER

The world keeps shrinking. Educators can take advantage of this fact when teachers reach across boundaries (physically or electronically) to learn with and from each other.

I have been very fortunate to have traveled widely for educational and personal purposes. During the course of these travels, I've discovered that educators around the world share many of the same concerns and can learn a great deal from one another's creativity in finding ways to teach all children and adults to read well.

Access to books, finding books that speak to children's interests and needs, preparing for high-stakes tests, and creating classrooms for learners are concerns of teachers around the globe. We also have so much to learn together. One of the best experiences we can have is to experience life in other countries. Attend an international conference sponsored by one of the major educational associations, IRA, NCTE, or Association for Supervision and Curriculum Development (ASCD).

DIGITAL-AGE CONNECTIONS

Classrooms and schools that connect with others across cyberspace create new forms of community that can be very powerful, too. I like the connections being made that help students experience other parts of the world firsthand.

One of the teachers in a local school visited Japan recently. She didn't want her students to lose out on the power of this cross-cultural experience so she arranged to communicate with them regularly via e-mail and also to send back pictures she took on her digital camera so the children could see what she was doing. In this way they all felt they had a real part of the trip. The teacher also connected with a school in Japan, and as a result the children in both schools shared their pictures and letters with one another, which made the world seem much smaller.

Students are now connecting via the Internet to discuss their responses to books they have all read. A Web site in Michigan, among other international projects available for school exchanges, is able to facilitate a dialogue among students in several countries. In this way, the joy of being able to share and hear others' responses to books brings literacy alive in a whole new way.

CONTINUING TO LOOK OUTWARD

The possibilities for connecting with teachers and students around the world keep expanding. Early in the 1970s, British educators stimulated us with ideas of more open classrooms, and then they introduced the idea of using little books for reading. Later the Inner London Teachers' Center model of involving students and parents in assessment processes stimulated us again. Where would we be without Reading Recovery, the program developed by Marie Clay with teachers in New Zealand? We have so adopted this program that many Americans forget the debt we owe to the folks down under in the antipodes.

We also gain insights into our educational system through international assessments. In the early 1990s, the International Education Study (Elly, 1992) indicated that the United States was in the top five countries for early literacy achievement. However, by the middle grades our students had dropped to the middle level in achievement among the developed nations. Our high school achievement in reading showed even further drops in international comparisons. As an extension of this international study of achievement, the Organisation for Economic Co-operation and Development (OECD) conducted a major study of literacy that was published in December 2001. This more extensive exploration of literacy development of 15-year-olds and literacy practices in schools provides added information about our school successes and where we can do better (OECD, 2001).

While not dealing with reading, the TIMMS mathematics results led to some careful analysis of how mathematics is taught in different countries (Germany, Japan, and the United States). Upon analysis of videotapes of actual lessons taught in the three countries, some basic differences emerged. The analysis revealed that Japanese teachers work together to solve instructional problems and spend several hours a week studying and working together. Teachers examine real lessons and analyze how best to work with students on the content. These comparisons have given educators a window through which to reflect on their own instructional practices and hopefully incorporate some of what was learned in better practices in the future.

We are part of a global community, and government and business leaders are focusing much attention on education because they know that the success of our students will determine our future. They will be working with counterparts who have been educated all over the world. Our roles as teachers and educators are critical in preparing children for the new realities we will all encounter. We must accept our roles as leaders in helping children become fully literate and comfortable members of the global community.

To Reflect

1. How do the ideas presented in Chapter 7 relate to your teaching experiences? What ideas support and confirm what you are already doing?

2. What did you find in this chapter that you can share with colleagues? Did something suggest new possibilities for your program?

3. What questions does this chapter raise for further discussion and reflection?

Bibliography

Allen, Rick. (2000). Before it's too late: Giving reading a last chance. Retrieved April 25, 2007 from http://www.ascd.org/video_demos/reading02/resources/reading1.html

Association for Supervision and Curriculum Development (Producer). (2000). The brain and reading [Videotape series]. Alexandria, VA: Association for Supervision and Curriculum Development.

Barton, B. (2000). *Telling stories your way: Storytelling and reading aloud in the classroom*. York, ME: Stenhouse.

Bell, N. (2003). *Visualizing and verbalizing: Stories*. San Louis Obispo, CA: Nancibell Inc/Gander Publishing.

Berthoff, A. E. (1987). The teacher as researcher. In D. Goswani & P. Stillman (Eds.), *Reclaiming the classroom: Teacher research as an agency for change* (pp. 28–38). Portsmouth, NH: Boynton/Cook.

Blachowicz, C., & Ogle, D. (2001). *Reading comprehension: Strategies for independent learners*. New York: Guilford Press.

Boran, K. (1999). *Rising from the ashes: A dramaturgical analysis of teacher change in a Chicago public high school after probation*. Unpublished doctoral dissertation, National-Louis University.

Burniske, R.W. (2000). *Literacy in the cyberage: Composing ourselves online*. Thousand Oaks, CA: Corwin Press.

Bush, G. (2003) The *School Buddy System: The Practice of Collaboration.* Chicago: American Library Association.

Bush, G. (2005). *Every Student Reads: Collaboration and Reading to Learn*. Chicago: American Association of School Librarians.

Calkins, L. (2001). *The art of teaching reading*. New York: Longman.

Carini, P. (1986). *Prospect's documentary process*. Bennington, VT: The Prospect School Center.

Carini, P. (2000). Prospect's descriptive process. In M. Himley & P. F. Carini (Eds.), *From another angle: Children's strengths and school standards/The Prospect center's descriptive review of the child* (pp. 8–22). New York: Teachers College Press.

Carr, E., & Ogle, D. (1987). K-W-L plus: A strategy for comprehension and summarization. *Journal of Reading, 30*, 626–631.

Carson, B. S. (with Murphey, C.). (1996). *Gifted hands*. Grand Rapids, MI: Zondervan Publishing.

Center for Improving Early Reading Achievement (CIERA). (2001). Retrieved January 8, 2007 from www.ciera.org

Center on English Learning & Achievement (CELA). (2000). Retrieved January 8, 2007 from www.cela.albany.edu

Cole, A. L. & Knowles, J. G. (2000) Researching teaching: Exploring teacher development through reflexive inquiry. Boston: Allyn & Bacon.

Collins, D. (1997). *Achieving your vision of professional development: How to assess your needs and get what you want.* Greensboro, NC: Serve.

Cooke, G. J. (2002). *Keys to success for urban school principals.* Thousand Oaks, CA: Corwin Press.

Cullinan, B. E. (2000). *Let's read about: Finding books they'll love to read* (2nd ed.). New York: Scholastic.

Cunningham, A. E., & Stanovich, K. E. (1998). What reading does for the mind. *American Educator,* (Spring–Summer), 8–17.

Cunningham, P., Hall, D., & Defee, M. (1998). Nonability-grouped, multilevel instruction: Eight years later. *Reading Teacher, 51*(8), 652.

Daniels, H. (2002). *Literature circles: Voice and choice in book clubs and reading groups.* Portland, ME: Stenhouse.

Darling-Hammond, L. (1996). *Teaching and America's future: Report of the National Commission and America's Future.* New York: National Commission on Teaching & America's Future.

Davey, B. (1983). Think aloud: Modeling the cognitive processes of reading comprehension. *Journal of Reading, 27,* 44–47.

Dillingofski, M. S. (1993). *Guidelines for teacher book discussion groups.* New York: American Association of Publishers.

Edwards, P., & Danridge, J. (2001). Developing collaboration with diverse parents. In V. Risko & K. Bromley (Eds.), *Collaboration for diverse learners: Viewpoints and practices* (pp. 251–274). Newark, DE: International Reading Association.

Edwards, P. A., Pleasants, H. M., & Franklin, S. H. (1999). *A path to follow: Learning to listen to parents.* Portsmouth, NH: Heinemann.

Elly, W. (1992). *International education study.* Newark, DE: International Reading Association.

Ferreiro, E., & Teberosky, A. (1982). *Literacy before schooling* (K. Goodman Castro, Trans.). Portsmouth, NH: Heinemann.

Fountas, I. C. (2001). *Guiding readers and writers grades 3–6: Teaching comprehension, genre, and content literacy.* Portsmouth, NH: Heinemann.

Fountas, I. C., & Pinnell, G. S. (1996). *Guided reading: Good first teaching for all children.* Portsmouth, NH: Heinemann.

Fry, E. (1977). Fry's readability graph: Clarifications, validity, and extension to level 17. *Journal of Reading, 21,* 242–253.

Gambrell, L., & Bales, R. (1986). Mental imagery and the comprehension-monitoring performance of fourth- and fifth-grade poor readers. *Reading Research Quarterly, 21,* 454–464.

Gelzheiser, L., & d'Angelo, C. (2000). Historical fiction and informational texts that support social studies standards: An annotated bibliography. *The Language and Literacy Spectrum: A Journal of the New York State Reading Association, 10,* 26–29.

Goleman, D. (1995). *Emotional intelligence. Why it can matter more than IQ.* New York: Bantam Books.

Graves, D., & Hansen, J. (1983). The author's chair. *Language Arts, 60,* 176–183.

Gurvitz, D. (1999). *Parent partnership for literacy.* Springfield, IL: IRC Conference.

Guthrie, J., Wigfield, A., & Von Secker, C. (2000). Effects of integrated instruction on motivation and strategy use in reading. *Journal of Educational Psychology, 92*(2), 331–341.

Habermas, J. (1979). *Communication and the evolution of society.* (T. McCarty, Trans.). Boston: Beacon Press.

Himley, M. & Carini P. F. (2000). *Another angle: Children's strengths and school standards: The prospect center's descriptive review of the child.* New York: Teachers College Press.

Hoffman, J. V. (1992). Critical reading/thinking across the curriculum: Using I-charts to support learning. *Language Arts, 69,* 121–127.

International Reading Association. (2000). Making a difference means making it different [Pamphlet]. Washington, DC: Author.

Johnson, D., & Johnson, R. (1990). *Cooperative learning warm ups, grouping strategies, and group activities.* Edina, MN: Interaction Book Company.

Johnson, F., Invernezzi, M., & Juel, C. (1998). *Book buddies: Guidelines for volunteer tutors of emergent and early readers.* New York: Guilford.

Kaser, S., & Short, K. (1997). Exploring cultural diversity through peer talk. In J. Paratore & R. McCormick (Eds.), *Peer talk in the classroom: Learning from research* (pp. 45–66). Newark, DE: International Reading Association.

Keene, E. O., & Zimmermann, S. (1997). *Mosaic of thought: Teaching comprehension in a reader's workshop.* Portsmouth, NH: Heinemann.

Kelly, M. (2000). *Of Dreams and New Realities: Mexican Immigrant Women in Transition.* Unpublished doctoral dissertation, National-Louis-University.

Kennedy, T., & Canney, G. (2001). Collaboration across language, age, and geographic borders. In V. Risko & K. Bromley (Eds.), *Collaboration for diverse learners: Viewpoints and practices* (pp. 310–329). Newark, DE: International Reading Association.

Kessler, R. (2000). *The soul of education: Helping students find connection, compassion, and character at school.* Arlington, VA: Association for Supervision and Curriculum Development.

Klooster, D., Steele, J., & Bloem, P. (2001). *Ideas without boundaries: International educational reform through reading and writing for critical thinking.* Newark, DE: International Reading Association.

Kropp, P. (1996). *How to make your child a reader for life.* New York: Broadway Books.

Lapp, D., Block, C. C., Cooper, E., Flood, J., Roser, N., & Tinajero, J. V. (2004). *Teaching all the children: Strategies for developing literacy in an urban setting.* New York: Guilford Press.

Lyons, C. (1998). Reading recovery in the United States: More than a decade of data. *Literacy, Teaching, and Learning: An International Journal of Early Literacy, K 1, 3,* 110–119.

Lytle, S., & Cochran-Smith, M. (1992). Communities for teacher research: Fringe or forefront? *American Journal of Education, 100*(3), 298–324.

McAllister, P. J. (1994). Using K-W-L for informal assessment. *The Reading Teacher, 47,* 6.

McTighe, J., & Lyman, F. T. Jr. (1988). Cueing thinking in the classroom. *Educational Leadership, 45*(7), 18–24.

Moll, L., Amanti, C., Neff, D., & Gonzalez, N. (1992). Funds of knowledge for teaching using a qualitative approach to connect homes and classrooms. *Theory into Practice, 31*(1), 132–137.

Morris, D. (2005). *TheHoward StreetTutoring manual: Teaching at-risk readers in the primary grades*. New York: Guilford.

Mulhall, C. (1997). Finding time for faculties to study together. *Journal of Staff Development, 18*(3), 29–31.

National Center for Educational Statistics. (2004). *National assessment of educational progress*. Washington, DC: U.S. Department of Education.

Neuman, S., Celano, D., Greco, A. N., & Shue, P. (2001). *Access for all: Closing the book gap for children in early education*. Newark,DE: International Reading Association.

Neuman, S. B., & Celano, D. (2001). Access to print in low-income and middle-income communities: An ecological study of four neighborhoods. *Reading Research Quarterly, 56*, 8–28.

Noddings, N. (1992). *The challenge to care in schools: An alternative approach to education*. New York: Teachers College Press.

Ogle, D. (1989). The know, want to know, learn strategy. In K. D. Muth (Ed.), *Children's comprehension of text: Research into practice* (pp. 205–223). Newark, DE: International Reading Association.

Ogle, D. (2000). Make it visual. In M. McLaughlin & M. E. Vogt (Eds.), *Creativity and innovation in content reading and learning* (pp. 103–114). Norwood, MA: Christopher Gordon.

Ogle, D. (2006). Best practices in adolescent literacy instruction. In L. Gambrell, L. Morrow, & M. Pressley (Eds.), *Best practices in literacy instruction* (3rd ed.) (pp. 127–156). New York: Guilford Press.

Ogle, D. M. (1986). K-W-L: A teaching model that develops active reading of expository text. *Reading Teacher, 40*, 564–570.

Ogle, D., & Fogelberg, E. (2001). Collaboration for change in reading instruction. In V. Risko & K. Bromley (Eds.), *Collaboration for diverse learners: Viewpoints and practices*. Newark, DE: International Reading Association.

Ogle, D., & Hunter, K. (2001). Developing leadership in literacy. In M. Bizar & R. Barr (Eds.), *School leadership in times of urban reform* (pp. 179–194). Mahwah, NJ: Lawrence Erlbaum.

Oldfather, P. (1995). Commentary: What's needed to maintain and extend motivation for literacy in the middle grades? *Journal of Reading, 38*, 420–422

Oldfather, P. (2002). Learning from students about overcoming motivation problems in literacy learning: A cross-study analysis and synthesis. *Reading and Writing Quarterly, 18*(4), 343–352.

Oldfather, P., & Dahl, K. (1994). Toward a social constructivist reconceptualization of intrinsic motivation for literacy learning. *Journal of Reading Behavior, 26*(2), 139–158.

Opitz, M. F., & Rasinski, T. V. (1998). *Good-by round robin: 25 effective oral reading strategies*. Portsmouth, NH: Heinemann.

Organisation for Economic Co-operation and Development. (2001). *The report of the PISA Study*. Washington, DC: Author.

Osborne, S. S., & Schulte, A. C. (2001). A school-university project on collaboration and consultation. In V. J. Risko & K. Bromley (Eds.), *Collaboration for diverse learners: Viewpoints and practices* (pp. 330–347). Newark, DE: International Reading Association.

Passman, R. (1999). *Discussion focusing on a developing student-centered practice with four middle-level school teachers.* Unpublished Doctoral Dissertation, National-Louis University.

Perez, B. (2001). Communicating and collaborating with linguistically diverse communities. In V. Risko & K. Bromley (Eds.), *Collaboration for diverse learners: Viewpoints and practices* (pp. 231–250). Newark, DE: International Reading Association,

Pressley, M. (2005). Best practices that work: Third edition: The case for balanced literacy. New York: Guilford.

Pressley, M., & Aflerbach, P. (1995). *Verbal reports of reading: The nature of constructively responsive reading.* Hillsdale, NJ: Erlbaum.

Quiroz, B.,Greenfield, P. M., & Alchech, M. (1999). Bridging cultures with a parent-teacher conference. *Educational Leadership, 56,* 68–70.

Raphael, T., & McMahon, S. I. (1994). Book club: An alternative framework for reading instruction. *The Reading Teacher, 48,* 102–116.

Rasinski, T., Blachowicz, C., & Lems, K. (2006). *Fluency instruction: Research-based best practices.* New York: Guilford.

Rasinski, T. V., Padak, N., Weible Church, B., Fawcett, G., Hendershot, J., Henry, J. M., Moss, B., Peck, J., Pryor, E. & Roskos, K.A. (Eds.) (2000). *Teaching comprehension and exploring multiple literacies: Strategies from the reading teacher.* Newark, DE: International Reading Association.

Risko, V., & Bromley, K. (Eds.). (2001). *Collaboration for diverse learners: Viewpoints and practices.* Newark, DE: International Reading Association.

Rodriguez-Brown, F. (2001). Home-school connections in a community where English is the second language: Project FLAME. In V. Risko & K. Bromley (Eds.), *Collaboration for diverse learners: Viewpoints and practices* (pp. 273–288). Newark, DE: International Reading Association.

Rogers, T., Tyson, C., Marshell, E. (2000). Living dialogues in one neighborhood: Moving toward understanding across discourses and practices of literacy and schooling. *Journal of Literacy Research, 30* (1), 1–24.

Sadoski, M, & Paivio, A. (2001). *Imagery and text: A dual coding theory of reading and writing.* Mahwah, NJ: Erlbaum Associates.

Schoenbach, R., Greenleaf, C., Cziko, C., & Hurwitz, L. (1999). *Reading for understanding: A guide to improving reading in middle and high school classrooms.* San Francisco: Jossey-Bass Publishers in partnership with WestEd.

Scholastic. (2006). Kids and family reading report. Retrieved September 20, 2006, from www.scholastic.com/readingreport

Short, K. G., & Harste, J. (with Burke, C.). (1996). *Creating classrooms for authors and inquirers* (2nd ed.). Portsmouth, NH: Heinemann.

Simone, G. (2001) Space to learn. *Educational Leadership, 59*(1), 66–70.

Smith, M. C. (2000) The real-world reading practices of adults. *Journal of Literacy Research, 32,* 25–32.

Smolan, R. (Ed.). (1986). *A day in the life of America.* New York: HarperCollins.

Stigler, J., & Hiebert, J. (1999). *The teaching gap: Best ideas from the world's teachers for improving education in the classroom.* New York: The Free Press.

Strickland, D. (1993). Networking for change: The Rutgers Literacy Curriculum Network. *Primary Voices K–6, 1*(2), 1– 3.

Sylwester, R. (1994). *A celebration of neurons: An educator's guide to the human brain.* Alexandria, VA: Association for Supervision and Curriculum Development.

Szymkoiak, D. (1998). Portfolio use in high school language arts classes. *Illinois Reading Council Journal, 23*(4), 15–21.

Taylor, B., Pearson, P. D., Clark, K., & Walpole, S. (2001). Effective schools: Accomplished teachers. Center for Improvement in Early Reading Achievement. Ann Arbor: University of Michigan. Retrieved November 2006, from www.cieral.org

Trealease, J. (2001). *The read-aloud handbook* (5th ed.). New York: Penguin.

Trealease, J. (2006). *The read-aloud handbook* (6th ed.). New York: Penguin.

Walpole, S., & McKenna, M. (2004). *The literacy coach's handbook.* New York: Guilford Press.

WestEd. (2000). *Teachers who learn, kids who achieve: A look at schools with model professional development.* San Francisco: Author.

Wilhelm, J. (2001). *Improving comprehension with think-aloud strategies: Modeling what good readers do.* New York: Scholastic.

Young, T. A., & Hadaway, N. L. (Eds.). (2006). *Supporting the literacy development of English learners: Increasing success in all classrooms.* Newark, DE: International Reading Association.

Zeigler, L. L., & Johns, J. L. (2004). *Using mental images: Visualization to strengthen comprehension.* Dubuque, IA: Kendall Hunt.

Zemelman, S., Bearden, P., Simmons, Y., & Leki P. (1999). *History comes home: Family stories across the curriculum.* Portland, ME: Stenhouse.

Index

CORWIN PRESS

The Corwin Press logo—a raven striding across an open book—represents the union of courage and learning. Corwin Press is committed to improving education for all learners by publishing books and other professional development resources for those serving the field of PreK–12 education. By providing practical, hands-on materials, Corwin Press continues to carry out the promise of its motto: **"Helping Educators Do Their Work Better."**